POCKET STUDY SKILLS

Series Editor: **Kate Williams**,
Oxford Brookes University, UK

Illustrations by Sallie Godwin

For the time-pushed student, the *Pocket Study Skills* pack a lot of advice into a little book. Each guide focuses on a single crucial aspect of study, giving you step-by-step guidance, handy tips and clear advice on how to approach the important areas which will continually be at the core of your studies.

Pocket Study Skills
Series Standing Order
ISBN 978-0230-21605-1
(outside North America only)

You can receive future titles in this series as they are published by placing a standing order. Please contact your bookseller or, in case of difficulty, write to us at the address below with your name and address, the title of the series and the ISBN quoted above.

Customer Services Department, Macmillan Distribution Ltd, Houndmills, Basingstoke, Hampshire RG21 6XS England

Published

14 Days to Exam Success

Blogs, Wikis, Podcasts and More

Brilliant Writing Tips for Students

Completing Your PhD

Doing Research

Getting Critical (2nd edn)

Planning Your Dissertation

Planning Your Essay (2nd edn)

Planning Your PhD

Posters and Presentations

Reading and Making Notes (2nd edn)

Referencing and Understanding Plagiarism

Reflective Writing

Report Writing

Science Study Skills

Studying with Dyslexia

Success in Groupwork

Time Management

Writing for University

POCKET STUDY SKILLS

Jeanne Godfrey

READING & MAKING NOTES

SECOND EDITION

palgrave
macmillan

First edition 2010
Second edition 2014

First published 2010 by
PALGRAVE MACMILLAN

Palgrave Macmillan in the UK is an imprint of Macmillan Publishers Limited, registered in England, company number 785998, of Houndmills, Basingstoke, Hampshire RG21 6XS.

Palgrave Macmillan in the US is a division of St Martin's Press LLC,
175 Fifth Avenue, New York, NY 10010.

Palgrave Macmillan is the global academic imprint of the above companies and has companies and representatives throughout the world.

Palgrave® and Macmillan® are registered trademarks in the United States, the United Kingdom, Europe and other countries.

ISBN: 978-1-137-40258-5 paperback

This book is printed on paper suitable for recycling and made from fully managed and sustained forest sources. Logging, pulping and manufacturing processes are expected to conform to the environmental regulations of the country of origin.

A catalogue record for this book is available from the British Library.

Printed in China

Contents

Acknowledgements   vii
Introduction   viii

Part 1 Now you are at university ... 1
1 Active reading and note making   1
2 Different reasons to read   7
3 Different reasons to make notes   13
  Summary   15

READING

Part 2 Reading for assignments 17
4 What your lecturers are looking for   17
5 Understand your assignment title   21
6 Take control of your reading list ...   25

7 ... and go beyond it?   34
8 Use reliable and academic sources   38
9 Fine-tune your selection   47
10 Write down the essentials   50
  Summary   52

Part 3 Decide *how* you are going to read 53
11 Three different ways to read   53
12 Plan the time to read   60
13 Create the right environment   62
  Summary   64

Part 4 Understand, question and evaluate what you read 65
14 Approach the text actively   65
15 Find the key message   66

16 Make up your own mind   83
17 Get the wider picture   88
18 What to do if you get stuck   90
    Summary   95

MAKING NOTES

Part 5 The essentials   97
19 Why bother making notes?   97
20 Key features of effective notes   100
21 Useful strategies and tips   104
22 Examples of good and poor
    notes   108
    Summary   113

Part 6 Match your method to
            your context   115
23 Different note-making formats   115
24 Making notes from lectures and
    audio-visual material   123
25 Tools, technology and note-
    making software   132
    Summary   139

Part 7 Make the most of your
            notes   141
26 Review and rework your notes   141
27 Things to be careful of when
    using your notes   145
    Summary   148
    Final comment   149

Appendix 1: Answers to exercise
on reliability of sources in Chapter 8   150

Appendix 2: Examples of common
abbreviations for note making   151

Appendix 3: Definitions of words
used in this guide   152

References   153

Useful resources   154

Index   155

Acknowledgements

My thanks go to all my students, past and present and future, for helping me develop insights into reading and making notes.

I am grateful to Kate Williams for asking me to write this book and for her continuing support. I would also like to thank Sallie Godwin for her excellent and humorous sketches, which really bring the text to life.

Thanks also to the Palgrave Macmillan team for their friendly and professional work with me on this book, particularly Suzannah Burywood and Caroline Richards.

The extract from the FSA report on nutritional labelling is reproduced with the kind permission of the National Heart Forum, and the article extract by A. Oswald is reproduced with the kind permission of Wiley-Blackwell Publishing.

Introduction

Reading and making notes form the foundations of a great deal of university study, and this pocket guide will take you quickly and clearly through the key points of these two activities. Confidence comes from knowing *what* to do and *how* to do it, but when you start out at university you may not know exactly what is expected of you. You may, for example, hold some of the common beliefs about university study listed below.

10 myths about reading and making notes at university

#1 You need to read most things on your reading list, starting at the top and working your way down.

#2 In your first year you will be reading and writing assignments rather than doing research.

#3 All books and articles are well written and truthful.

#4 You should read academic texts carefully from start to finish.

#5 There is only one correct way to understand a text.

#6 You can't really disagree with an academic text because you are not an expert in that subject.

#7 If you don't understand something or feel confused, it is probably because you are being a bit thick.

#8 Intelligent people and good readers usually only need to read things once.

#9 You should look up all the words you don't understand as you go along.

#10 Good notes should have all the points from the text copied down.

This pocket guide will explode these myths one by one. It will tell you exactly what your university tutors *do* expect of you and what you need to do to meet these expectations. I want you to be able to hit the ground running from the very start of your studies, to get the best marks possible for your work, and to make the best possible use of your talents, your tutors and your time.

No matter what your starting point is, you could probably read and make notes more effectively by adjusting or adding to your current reading strategies. This guide gives you practical advice and uses real assignment titles, reading lists and text extracts. It also looks at real tutor feedback and university marking criteria.

Reading for study can actually be an enjoyable experience, and I hope that using this pocket guide will help you to feel more confident and relaxed about this aspect of your work.

Active reading and note making

Below is a table that summarises the differences in approach between reading and making notes at school/college and degree-level reading and making notes.

School/college	University
The reading material is usually set, prioritised and managed by the teacher.	Apart from a few key texts, *you* are expected to decide what to read and what not to read.
	(*Text* is a general term for any type of written document – e.g. a book, article, report, course textbook. *Text* can also be used to describe speech or something visual.)

School/college	University
Generally, all students read the same texts.	Because of the choices you make, some or all of the texts you read will be different from those of other students on your course, even for the same assignment.
Students learn mainly by absorbing the information in the texts and repeating it in different forms.	You are expected to think beyond the information in the texts and to make up your own mind about *whether* the information is important, *why* it is important and *how* it connects with other information and ideas.
Although there are different reasons for making notes, the main purpose is to record information and ideas.	At university there is a much wider range of reasons for making notes: for example, to jot down your own ideas on a topic, to record the details of an academic journal you have found or to make notes on your evaluation of an argument the author has put forward.
	Importantly, a key purpose of note making is to help you produce and record a clear picture, not only of what you have understood but also of your analysis and evaluation of what you have read, seen or listened to.

Having an active approach

At university you are expected to develop what is called an active approach to study, and in order to do this you need to have the right tools for the job. The first tool in your study toolkit is to be aware of the main purposes of reading and note making outlined above. The

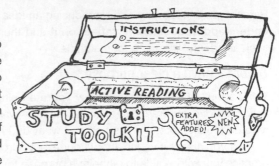

second tool in the box is to understand in a bit more detail what an 'active approach to study' means.

Active reading and note making means that instead of passively reading and noting down, you **engage your brain and think about** the information **before, during and after** reading and making notes.

Although you might need to memorise information for some exams, your tutors generally want much more than an assignment sprinkled with remembered ideas and quotations. At university your tutors expect you to form your own informed views about a text, including how it connects with other texts and with your own ideas and knowledge.

Rather than just learning and reproducing an idea or piece of information, you should **understand it, question it, reflect on it** and then **apply it to a particular purpose,** such as addressing an assignment title.

Before – have a clear purpose

Think about *whether*, *why* and *how* you are going to read something, and *whether*, *why* and *how* you are going to make notes. Always ask yourself: 'Why am I going to read and make notes on this text and what do I hope to produce at the end?' Don't worry if you are a bit vague about your exact purpose at the start of your course; with practice you will be able to pinpoint a purpose for reading a text.

Before – make predictions

Before you start to read something in detail, make some predictions about what you expect to find. Predictions and expectations (even if they turn out to be wrong) will help engage your brain.

During – build a scaffold

Always try to link what you read to what you already know about the subject, how it relates to other topics and how it relates to your own life experience. This is important, as you need to build a 'knowledge scaffold' in your mind onto which you can attach new information.

During – challenge the author

Someone wrote each text you read. Think about who they are, why they might have written their text and what you think they hoped to achieve. As you read, question and challenge the author in your mind.

During – engage and enjoy

Engage and interact with the text – there should be a continuous two-way process of reading and thinking, and of putting together old and new information to create your own unique way of thinking. React to what you read – you will enjoy it much more!

After – review it and use it

Once you have read and made notes on something, don't just put it away, never to look at it again. Review, rework, use and reuse what you have learnt and noted.

Building up your reading stamina

Reading and making notes actively and purposefully is hard work and you will probably find it difficult at first. Don't forget that the experts in the field (including your lecturers) will have read and written about the same subjects for years, and so will have developed large scaffolds which allow their brains to easily fit new information into what they already know.

Have the confidence to know that you too will gradually develop scaffolds and build up your subject knowledge. Texts that at first seem almost impossibly difficult and alien will become easier as you go forward, but only if you build up your 'reading muscles' by – you guessed it – reading. If you are finding reading a challenge, read little but often rather than in long sessions. Parts 3 and 4 give you specific strategies for building up your reading stamina.

Studying effectively involves having a clear purpose before you start reading or making notes. You might think that the main reading purpose at university is to understand information in order to use it directly in exams and assignments, but, happily, things are not as dull or as simple as that. There are many different reasons why you might want to read, including for interest and enjoyment.

Part 2 of this book will focus on reading for assignments, but it is worth first looking briefly at the other reasons to read at university. Below is a list of reasons accompanied by some useful points and examples, using law as a subject area. Spend a few minutes thinking about how the different reading purposes apply to you and your subject area – you might be able to add to the list. Most of the different types of reading you do will feed directly or indirectly into your assignments but are worthwhile even if they don't, because doing assignments is only part of the process of being interested in your subject and of engaging with it at a deep level.

Reasons to read

For interest and enjoyment

This is always good to do, but make a time management plan so that you leave yourself enough space for course and assignment-focused reading.

Example reading sources:

Legal sections in quality daily newspapers, online global networks and interest groups, *The Lawyer*, *New Law Journal*, *Lawyer Monthly*, legal novels (thriller, crime, historical), interesting books and articles on your course reading list.

To widen your knowledge of a topic or issue

It is good to do lots of this during your first year and to ask your tutors what general reading they would recommend. Even before you get to university you can ask for a course reading list.

Example reading sources:

The sources on your reading list marked 'essential' or 'basic'. Course textbooks and introductory books.

To understand a particular concept, term, theory or model

It is important that you accurately understand particular concepts, terms and theories; do not skip over these and carry on with only a vague or guessed idea of what a term means. You need to be able to understand and practise using concepts and ideas so that you feel comfortable using them in seminars, discussion, presentations and your own writing.

Example reading sources:

Your course and introductory textbooks (these will usually have an explanatory glossary at the back). Subject-specific dictionaries, e.g. *A Dictionary of Law*, *Dictionary of Legal Usage*. Online sources such as Wikipedia (although remember that this is not always a reliable source of correct information).

To learn about different perspectives on an issue

To do this you need to be able to recognise the difference between description, explanation, argument and opinion (see pp. 70–2). You also need to know how to select sources that focus on discussing different perspectives. Textbooks will give an overview of different viewpoints, but you also need to find the books and journal articles that contain the actual arguments and discussions. Journal article abstracts will help you identify which articles contain an argument – look for phrases such as *'we argue / propose / suggest / assert that …'* You can also ask your tutor for advice on relevant sources.

Example reading source:

Walker L and Monahan J (1988). Social facts: scientific methodology as legal precedent. *California Law Review* 76(4), 877–96.

To analyse (break down) and evaluate evidence, ideas or arguments

This is one of the most important university reading purposes. We will look at what is called 'reading critically' in Chapter 16.

Example reading sources:

Just about everything!

To find evidence and arguments that support your own viewpoint

This is another key reading purpose. Importantly, you can only develop a strong argument if you have first analysed and evaluated all the evidence and *other* points of view. Make sure that the sources you use to support your own point are reliable (see pp. 38–43).

To memorise information for an exam

You may not need to do as much of this as you think. If you are unsure, check with your tutor so that you don't waste time memorising things unnecessarily.

As lecture and seminar preparation or follow-up

It's important to make the most of your lecture and seminar time, and you will get much more out of this if you do some reading both beforehand and afterwards. Preparatory reading will help you understand what the lecturer is talking about and so leave you more time for thinking, contributing, making notes or asking questions during the session. After the lecture or seminar, going over any notes you have made and any slides or handouts will help you to develop your understanding, remember key points and create new ideas.

To find your own research topic

This is an important function, particularly in final-year undergraduate and postgraduate work. Remember that in order to find your own angle on an issue or to identify an interesting area for your project and research, you first need to have built up your knowledge of your subject and of its various models and arguments.

To look at the structure, style and vocabulary of a text

You don't have to look at a text solely for its style and vocabulary but it's a useful thing to do sometimes as you read for other reasons.

To edit and proofread your own work

This is an important reading function that students sometimes overlook. Reading and rereading your own work several times before you hand it in is likely to lead to significantly higher marks.

3 Different reasons to make notes

As outlined in Chapter 1, active note making means thinking about *why* you want to make notes and what you want to do with them afterwards. Notes include any type of jotting down, pictures, scribbles, drafts or other forms of rough writing you produce.

In terms of reading, your notes should help you achieve your reading purpose (widening your knowledge, finding a research topic etc.). Below is a list of different things you can do to help you achieve your objective.

Different things to focus on according to your purpose

1 Notes you can make *before* you start reading:
- predictive questions and ideas – what you already know and think about the topic and what you think the text might or might not say.

2 Notes you can make only *while* you are reading:
- a record of the key points
- the reference details of sources mentioned in the text or in the end bibliography.

3 **Notes you can make *before*, *during* or *after* reading:**
   ▶ your own understanding (using your own words) of the text's key points
   ▶ notes on how your own knowledge and experience relates to what the text says
   ▶ random, creative thoughts and ideas on the topic
   ▶ points and ideas that form the development of your own argument
   ▶ points and ideas that can form the basis of a report or essay plan
   ▶ ideas for your own project or research
   ▶ a list of questions, things to investigate further, look up or discuss with other students and/or tutors
   ▶ words or phrases you don't fully understand in order to look them up later.

4 **Notes you can make *after* reading:**
   ▶ your own summary and reflection in your own words of the key points in the text
   ▶ your own thoughts on how ideas/information from different sources connect or contrast.

Something to mention here is that you don't have to make specific types of notes at specific stages – in fact, it is often a good idea to read a text and get a general understanding of it before making any notes.

If you don't usually make notes, you might like to at least experiment with doing so (see Parts 5 and 6) – you may find that making notes improves your performance.

Summary

- Take responsibility for your own learning from the start.

- The point of reading and making notes at university is to allow you to come to your own independent understanding of your subject.

- Having an active approach to study means deciding *whether*, *why* and *how* to read and make notes, and being engaged *before*, *during* and *after* reading.

- Having a clear goal for your reading and note making will increase your motivation, which will in turn increase your level of understanding and thus your enjoyment.

- Your tutors give you assessed and non-assessed tasks to see whether you have understood the point of an issue or question, and to see whether you have engaged with it at a deep level. Reading for reasons such as widening your subject knowledge, preparing for a lecture or even just rereading your own work all help develop your understanding and way of thinking about your subject.

- Reading actively is hard work and if your brain hurts a bit, this probably means you are doing it right!

- The only way to build up your active reading muscles is to practise active reading.

Producing an excellent assignment is a bit like building a house – first you need to understand your design brief (your assignment title) and then you must build your house brick by brick, using good quality materials (reliable sources) and good workmanship (good quality thinking and appropriate writing style).

The diagram on the next page uses this building analogy to show how you need to build upwards from the solid foundation of understanding your assignment title.

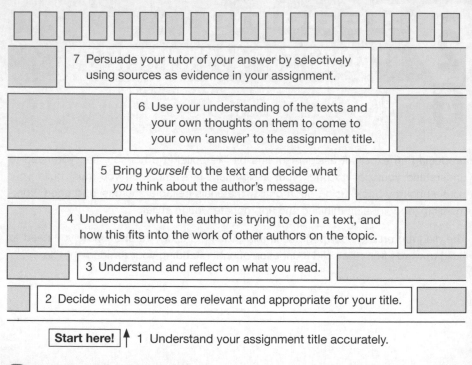

7 Persuade your tutor of your answer by selectively using sources as evidence in your assignment.

6 Use your understanding of the texts and your own thoughts on them to come to your own 'answer' to the assignment title.

5 Bring *yourself* to the text and decide what *you* think about the author's message.

4 Understand what the author is trying to do in a text, and how this fits into the work of other authors on the topic.

3 Understand and reflect on what you read.

2 Decide which sources are relevant and appropriate for your title.

Start here! ↑ 1 Understand your assignment title accurately.

Lecturers might use more formal language to describe these bricks. On the next page, grouped into the seven stages, are extracts from real lecturer feedback and from real university marking criteria for excellent and for poor work. Make sure your work takes account of these stages so that you build a wall that is strong!

✓   ✗

	Good work	Poor work
7	'Evaluates evidence and synthesises materials clearly to develop persuasive arguments.' 'Evidence used appropriately to support their conclusion.'	'Baseless assertions.' 'Essay is over-reliant on too few sources.' 'Poorly used material.'
6	'... clear insight and independent thought.' 'An accurate and critically reflective treatment of all the main issues.'	'Uses mainly description rather than coming to a critical conclusion.'
5	'... willingness to engage critically with the literature and ability to go beyond it ...' '... mindful of other interpretations ...'	'... does not go beyond the assertion of points derived from the literature.'
4	'... clear understanding of the nature of the material.' '... ability to analyse materials and their implications.'	'... lack of awareness of the context of the material.'
3	'Sources used accurately and concisely but do not dominate...' '... good command of the literature ...'	'inaccurate reading and limited understanding ...'
2	'... evidence of ability to select appropriately ...' '... detailed *and* broad knowledge base.'	'Needs to refer to the relevant literature.' 'Some sources used are not academically rigorous.'
1	'Has interpreted the question fully and accurately.'	'... has not clearly understood the assignment task.'

5 Understand your assignment title

Understanding your assignment title is fundamental. Don't make the mistake of reading the title quickly, assuming you know what it means and then plunging into unfocused reading. Not understanding the title properly is a common cause of low assignment marks.

> ✓ 'has interpreted the question fully and accurately'
> ✗ 'has not clearly understood the assignment task'

For your assignment title, make sure you have clearly identified and understood:

C: the **concept** words or phrases – words related to the content of the topic.
F: the **function** words – does the title ask you to describe, analyse, argue, or some of these things together?
S: the **scope** of the title – what you are asked to cover and not to cover. If the scope is not explicit in the title, you will need to decide on the scope yourself.

Use these three aspects to break down and to carefully analyse your title. Discuss it with fellow students and get advice from your tutor if you are still not sure what it means.

Let's have a look at two real assignment titles and see how the student has used the three aspects C, F and S to understand them.

Assignment title 1

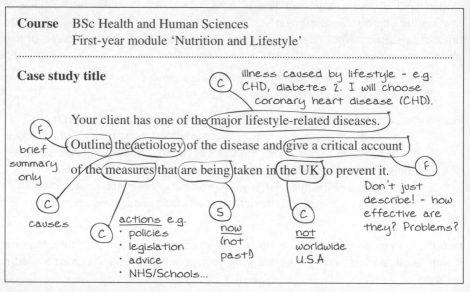

Course BSc Health and Human Sciences
First-year module 'Nutrition and Lifestyle'

Case study title

(C) illness caused by lifestyle - e.g. CHD, diabetes 2. I will choose coronary heart disease (CHD).

Your client has one of the major lifestyle-related diseases.

(F) brief summary only

Outline the aetiology of the disease and give a critical account of the measures that are being taken in the UK to prevent it.

(F) Don't just describe! - how effective are they? Problems?

(C) causes

(C) actions e.g.
· policies
· legislation
· advice
· NHS/Schools...

(S) now (not past!)

(C) not worldwide U.S.A

Assignment title 2

Course   MSc in Economic Psychology
Seminar on 'Happiness and the Economy'

Essay title

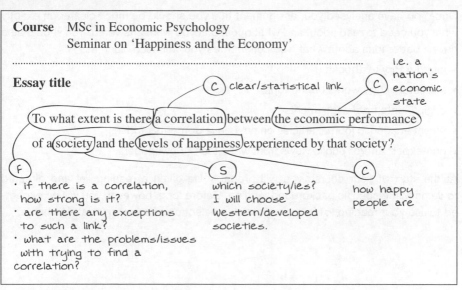

(C) clear/statistical link

(C) i.e. a nation's economic state

To what extent is there (a correlation) between (the economic performance) of a (society) and the (levels of happiness) experienced by that society?

(F)
· if there is a correlation, how strong is it?
· are there any exceptions to such a link?
· what are the problems/issues with trying to find a correlation?

(S) which society/ies? I will choose Western/developed societies.

(C) how happy people are

For more help with assignment titles, see *Planning Your Essay* and *Getting Critical* in this series.

A clearer idea of what you need

Once you have analysed your assignment title you should be much clearer on exactly what you need to read about and what questions you want answered. You should also have a better idea about what *types* of sources you will need, such as:

▶ introductory textbooks
▶ key established works on the topic
▶ original data from experiments
▶ recent academic journal articles on new developments or ideas
▶ non-expert and/or public views from websites or newspapers.

At the start of your course you will probably be given a reading list and directed towards some specific background reading. Before long, however, you will be expected to use your reading list to make your own selection of sources for assignments.

> **Myth #1** You need to read most things on your reading list, starting at the top and working your way down.

Now that you have analysed your assignment title, you can approach your reading list in a purposeful way and decide what *you* want to read rather than letting your reading list control you. Your tutors do not want you to read everything on the reading list – they want to see that you can *discriminate* between sources (i.e. make good judgements) and to see an '... ability to select appropriately ...'.

Myth #2 In your first year you will be reading and writing assignments rather than doing research.

In fact, selecting and finding sources is a key form of academic research, and the uniqueness of your assignment starts when you make your own selection of sources. Being able to select appropriate sources from your reading list is also necessary for most other reading purposes.

Let's look at a section from the reading list for the 'Nutrition and Lifestyle' module and see how you might assess whether any of the sources listed are relevant for assignment 1 on p. 22. Remember that the focus of the assignment is to critically evaluate the measures that are being taken to prevent a lifestyle disease (in this case, coronary heart disease).

> **!** **Attention!** Notice that the lecturers do not always give the complete bibliographic details of the texts in their reading lists – you will be expected to complete these details yourself and you must always use the full bibliographic details of any source for your assignment bibliography and reference list. For more on how to reference, see *Referencing and Understanding Plagiarism* in this series.

Reading list for 'Nutrition and Lifestyle' module

The reading list below is for the module in general. You will need more specific readings for your chosen topic (please see departmental Key Texts collection and ask your tutor for guidance if necessary).

Tutor's annotations – these give clues to relevant reading. Take the tutor's advice, and for your specific topic (CHD), look through the collection of Key Texts and ask your tutor for advice on other sources.

The latest editions of *MAFF Manual of Nutrition*, MAFF Manual of Nutrition, Food Standards Agency, London.

The FSA (Food Standards Agency): www.food.gov.uk/

Scientific Advisory Committee on Nutrition (SACN): www.sacn.gov.uk

Scan these websites for latest government recommendations on dietary advice for preventing CHD.

Bray GA (2006). Obesity: the disease. *Journal of Medicinal Chemistry* 49(14), 4001–7.

Scan this article to see if any sections look at the links between lifestyle, obesity and CHD.

Fisher M (ed.) (2004). *Heart disease and diabetes.* London: Martin Dunitz.

Garrow JS, James WPT and Ralph A (eds) (2000). *Human nutrition and dietetics.* Note – 10th edition.

These two books have editors (ed.) and chapters written by different authors – common in the academic world. Select only relevant chapters. Key authors often write chapters in edited books that give a condensed version of their longer work – very useful!

Gibney MJ, Vorster H and Kok FJ (2002). *Introduction to human nutrition.* Oxford: Blackwell Publishing.

Introductory textbook – you will only need to quickly scan and read the parts that look at nutrition-based causes of CHD.

McArdle W, Katch V and Katch F (2006). *Nutrition for sport and exercise.*

What you need to eat for sport. Not relevant to your assignment topic.

Mozaffarian D, Hao T, Rimm EB, Willett WC and Hu FB (2011). Changes in diet and lifestyle and long-term weight gain in women and men. *New England Journal of Medicine* 364(25), 2392–404.

Not directly relevant.

So, from this section of the reading list there are just two websites and a total of three or four sections from the other seven texts that would be relevant for an assignment on coronary heart disease and preventative measures.

You will probably need to find a few other sources yourself. Look at the assignment title again – what reading gaps do you need to fill? You still need some sources on preventative measures other than nutrition (e.g. exercise) and also some sources that give different evaluative viewpoints on the effectiveness of these measures.

Let's now take a quick look at the complete reading list for the MSc Economic Psychology seminar (assignment 2 on p. 23), and decide which sources are likely to be relevant for possible links between economic performance and happiness. Remember that in tutor reading lists some of the bibliographic entries may be incomplete.

Reading list for 'Happiness and the Economy' seminar

Basic reading

The tutor has been helpful, directing you to specific chapters or library catalogue numbers (2.930), and telling you which sources are held in the department (Box).

Argyle M (2001). *The psychology of happiness*. Departmental box.

← Not directly relevant – just scan.

Easterlin RA (2006). Life cycle happiness and its sources: intersections of psychology, economics, and demography. *Journal of Economic Psychology* 27(4), 463–82.

← The section of this article that discusses *economics* will be relevant.

EITHER

Myers (1994). Who is happy – and why? (Chapter 11 of *Exploring Social Psychology*) 2.930.

OR

Myers and Diener (1995). Who is happy? *Psychological Science* 6(1), 10–19.

← Might be relevant – scan to check, keeping your focus on economic performance and happiness. Take tutor's advice – you only need one text or the other. Note that these refs are quite old – ask your tutor why they are on the reading list.

Lyubomirsky S (2001). Why are some people happier than others? The role of cognitive and motivational processes in well-being. *American Psychologist* 56(3), 239.

Might be relevant – scan to check, keeping your focus on economic performance and happiness.

Additional material

Anielski M (2007). *The economics of happiness: building genuine wealth*. Canada: New Society Publishers.

Looks directly relevant but you might not need to read it all.

Bruni L (ed.) (2008). *Handbook on the economics of happiness*. Edward Elgar Publishing.

Looks directly relevant and useful for an overview and further sources. Might not need to read it all. NB: '*ed.*' means *editor*.

Graham C (2010). The challenges of incorporating empowerment into the HDI: some lessons from happiness economics and quality of life research. *Human Development Reports Research Paper* 13. United Nations.

Not directly relevant because it focuses on empowerment, but probably worth a scan.

Kaplan (1987). Lottery winners: the myth and the reality. *J Gamb Beh* 3, 168–78.

Not relevant. Individual wealth via winning the lottery does not directly relate to the general economy.

MacKerron G (2012). Happiness economics from 35,000 feet. *Journal of Economic Surveys* 26(4), 705–35.

◄ Looks directly relevant.

Oswald AJ (1997). Happiness and economic performance. *The Economic Journal* 107(445), 1815–31.

◄ Looks directly relevant but the text is relatively old.

So, from this reading list you would need to just scan three and to read one section of one text from the 'basic reading' group. You would probably also want to read four of the six texts under 'additional material'. This might sound like a lot but it is Master's level, and you would want to select only relevant sections from these texts. You would probably also need to find one or two other sources of your own.

Some other things to remember about reading lists

▶ You may get a thorough and helpful reading list or you may not – some lecturers expect you to do more detective work than others.
▶ Even with the 'required' or 'essential' reading section there may be titles that cover similar ground, so still be selective.
▶ If you want to ask your lecturer for guidance, don't expect them to tell you what to read. Do some thinking first and then ask your lecturer to comment on your choices.
▶ Reflect, even if briefly, on *all* the titles on your list, even the ones you reject – this will help you become familiar with authors and topics in the subject.
▶ Discuss sources with your fellow students – you're supposed to share references.

If the library doesn't have a copy of something you want ...

Don't panic. This is quite common, as few libraries can have enough copies for all students at all times. As we have seen, most reading lists will give you acceptable alternatives and you will find further similar titles through your own search. Reserve the title if it's out on loan and ask if there are any other university libraries you can use. You can also get advice from your tutor or other students and check online sites, bookshops and student notices for second-hand copies.

If you think you have a good range of suitable sources already, trying to find more just for the sake of it will be a waste of time. Stick to the rule of only searching for something if you have a clear idea of what you are looking for and why. Remember that your tutors want to see 'evidence of ability to select *appropriately*'.

However, if done well and for the right reasons, going off-road will help you build up a 'good command of the literature' and will also gain you marks.

The two most important points to check when you are doing your own source search for an assignment is that **your sources are specific and reliable.**

We will look at source reliability in Chapter 8. Let's concentrate for now on finding sources that are as specific as possible. From the 'Nutrition and Lifestyle' module reading list on pp. 27–8 we identified that we still needed sources that contained a critical evaluation of the measures being taken to prevent heart disease in the UK. Below is a selection of off-road sources a student found by using the search phrase 'effectiveness of preventative measures for CHD in the UK'. In the right-hand column are 'yes /no' comments about the source's relevance to this topic.

Off-road sources found for assignment 1

Ananthaswamy A (2004). Eat less and keep disease at bay. *New Scientist* 2444, 11–12.

'Disease' is *too general* and not about eating less as a measure being taken – no.

Bupa (2010). *Call for government intervention to reduce levels of heart disease*. http://www.bupa.co.uk/ individuals/health-information/health-news-index/2010/hi-250610-heart-disease-intervention [Accessed 26 January 2014]

About CHD and why and whether the govt. is taking steps to prevent it – yes.

Davies R, Roderick P and Raftery J (2003). The evaluation of disease prevention and treatment using simulation models. *European Journal of Operational Research* 150(1), 53–66. [Accessed 26 January 2014]

This is about disease in general and comparison of different data simulation models – no.

Gemmell RF and Heller K et al. (2006). Potential population impact of the UK government strategy for reducing the burden of coronary heart disease in England: comparing primary and secondary prevention strategies. *Qual Saf Health Care* 15(5), 339–43. [Accessed 23 January 2014]

About potential population impact, not efficacy of preventative measures, so not directly relevant –no.

Health Development Agency (no date). *Coronary heart disease: guidance for implementing the preventive aspects of the National Service Framework.* http://www.nice.org.uk/niceMedia/documents/chdframework.pdf [Accessed 23 January 2014]

About what measures the govt. is taking to prevent CHD and how to implement them, although it will not contain an evaluation of the measures – yes.

National Health Service (2011). *Coronary heart disease – prevention*. http://www.nhs.uk/Conditions/coronary-heart-disease/Pages/prevention.aspx [Accessed 23 January 2014]

Advice about preventative measures (but probably no evaluation of them) – yes.

UK Essays (no date). *Prevention of CHD in the Indian population*. http://www.ukessays.co.uk/essays/nursing/prevention-of-chd.php [Accessed 26 January 2014]

Preventative measures in India not the UK – no.

Use reliable and academic sources

Myth #3 All books and articles are well written and truthful.

Let's now look at reliability. At university it is *your* responsibility to check the reliability of your sources – in other words, you need to check that you can trust what your sources say. Make sure that:

▶ you know who wrote something and that they are an **authority** on their topic. Anonymous sources are much more likely to be of poor quality and/or contain incorrect information.

▶ your sources are **up to date** (current). You will want to read older sources, but check that you also have the most current information on the topic.

▶ the source is likely to be **accurate and balanced** and that you are aware of possible bias. For example, political reports and newspaper articles may not give a balanced and objective view.

▶ you are aware of what 'reliable' means for the type of information you need. For example, if you need information about public opinion on a topic, then opinion polls, newspapers and TV programmes will be reliable sources for this information.

▶ you get hold of the original (primary) source of information where possible because something reported second- or third-hand will probably be less accurate and reliable. Find the original experiment, data or article rather than another report or article (a secondary source) that discusses the primary material. In reality, you will often use secondary sources, but you will usually also be expected to read the key primary texts on a topic.

What is an academic source?

❌ 'Some sources used are not academically rigorous.'

For most assignments you will need to use sources that are not only reliable but are also regarded as *academic*. This means sources written by experts (or authorities) that have gone through a peer-review process – when the book or article has been sent to other experts for checking before publication. Peer-reviewed sources are reliable and are also described as academic, reputable or authoritative.

Books published by an established publisher will usually have been sent to expert reviewers before publication. Articles published in a journal described as 'academic' or 'scholarly' means that the journal uses peer review and so will be reliable, but you should check a journal's background if you are unsure. It doesn't matter whether a journal is in print, online or both – what matters is that it has been peer reviewed.

Reports from government departments and other established organisations such as the WHO or EU Commission are usually seen as reliable and the team of authors often includes academics. Such reports are not strictly scholarly because they have not been peer reviewed, but they are authoritative. Bear in mind that reports are commissioned by someone and might contain bias.

Source types that are *not* academically rigorous include:
- academic conference proceedings
- newspapers (even long articles in quality papers such as *The Times* or the *Guardian*)
- magazines (even quality magazines such as the *Economist*, *Newsweek* and *New Scientist*)
- trade publications and company websites
- publications and websites of charities, and of campaign or pressure groups
- student theses or essays
- Wikipedia articles.

Always check your online sources

▶ Some online databases contain only peer-reviewed academic journals but some of them (even one that describes itself as a 'research database') also contain newspapers, magazines and trade publications.

▶ Although subject gateways (directories) such as such as Intute, DOAJ, HighWire, Zetoc Ingenta, Copac, Pinakes and Scirus are more academically reliable, you should still check any material you find. Read the description of a database or gateway before you go into it – what does it say it contains? You may be able to google it and/or get a description of its publications on the 'home' or 'about us' page.

▶ Online search engines (Google, Alta Vista, Yahoo, Wolframalpha etc.) will obviously give you both reliable and unreliable material but you also need to check material you find through Google Scholar as it will include magazines and student theses.

▶ Wikipedia is a type of encyclopaedia and is therefore only a basic summary. It is a secondary or even tertiary source, is anonymous and is not peer reviewed – all things that make it unreliable and not academic. Wikipedia may be useful for some initial definitions and to give you links to other sources but you should not use it as an actual source in your assignment.

- Always check that you know the author of any website you use. Who funds and supports the site? Is the purpose of the site made clear? Is any advertising clearly distinguished from the main text?

- Words such as *research journal* or *volume/issue number* are being increasingly used on unreliable and non-academic websites so don't rely on such descriptions.

- Words that should warn you that an online website or article is not academic are: *magazine*, *digest*, *personals*, *news*, *press release*, *correspondent*, *journalist*, *special report, company*, *classified* and *advertisement*.

So, with reliability (authority, currency and accuracy) and academic rigour in mind, have another look at some of the off-road sources found for assignment 1, listed again below. Decide whether each source is unreliable, reliable but not academic, or reliable and academic. Answers are on p. 150.

	Your comments on reliability
Ananthaswamy A (2004). Eat less and keep disease at bay. *New Scientist* 2444, 11–12.	

	Your comments on reliability
Davies R, Roderick P and Raftery J (2003). The evaluation of disease prevention and treatment using simulation models. *European Journal of Operational Research* 150(1), 53–66. [Accessed 26 January 2014]	
Health Development Agency (no date). *Coronary heart disease: guidance for implementing the preventive aspects of the National Service Framework.* http://www.nice.org.uk/niceMedia/documents/chdframework.pdf [Accessed 26 January 2014]	
UK Essays (no date). *Prevention of CHD in the Indian population.* http://www.ukessays.co.uk/essays/nursing/prevention-of-chd.php [Accessed 26 January 2014]	

Make the most of your library

With so much information available online, some students don't go near their university library until the end of their second year or later. This is a shame because your library can help you with some of the very problems that arise from information overload. Don't make the mistake of thinking that the internet is just like a big online library – it isn't!

Go to your library and ask for a demonstration of how the catalogue system works, which books and journals are available online, and what the short loan section contains. Find out how many items you can take out at once, how to reserve a book and details of late return penalties.

The table below compares the advantages and disadvantages of using your university library and doing your own internet search. It ends with a space for you to note down your own additional thoughts.

Searching for sources using library resources and staff

Pros:

Material has already been pre-selected by lecturers and library staff for its importance, relevance, reliability and academic quality.

The intranet and library catalogue material (again, chosen by your tutors/library) is more likely to be reliable than material from the internet.

Library staff are there to help you with selecting and finding texts.

Has an online catalogue system that contains a list of all its resources. Will also give you free access to other academic online databases.

You can use the 'sort' facility of the library catalogue to put sources in order of publication.

Will have primary printed material and back copies of journals, newspapers and magazines that are not available online.

Will have specialist dictionaries, study guides and material written by your university not available online.

Provides a quiet and comfortable environment in which to study, away from distractions.

Free Wifi connection and use of DVDs.

Free use of magazines and newspapers, dictionaries, encyclopaedias and other print material.

Staff will be able to arrange for you to borrow from other libraries.

Cons:

The copies of a book or article may be out on loan (but you can reserve them!).

Searching for sources using only the internet

Pros:

A huge number of sources are available.

24-hour access (although your library may also be open 24 hours).

Cons:

Search engines will often return a large number of returns and false matches and it can be hard to find the most relevant source.

Sometimes difficult to find out who wrote something and whether the source is reliable and peer reviewed.

A significant number of academic sources are not yet available online.

You often have to pay for downloads of complete books or articles.

Your own thoughts on the pros and cons of using the library vs. the internet

9 Fine-tune your selection

This is an important stage that will save you a great deal of time. Collect your selection of sources and give each one a job interview. Does it have the correct expertise, qualifications and experience for what you want it to do?

Read the title, contents page, headings and sub-headings and go through the index to narrow down the sections that are specifically relevant to your needs. Quickly scan through the text, giving yourself a time limit. If you can't find the points you are looking for in the first 10–15 minutes then the text is probably not directly relevant.

You may feel that deciding not to read something is somehow being disrespectful to the author, but this is just how academic study works – you are simply identifying that what the author has written is not right for this particular job.

Reviews, abstracts and summaries

These are all useful in different ways to give you a general idea of a text, but remember that if you decide to use the source in your assignment you will need to read the text itself in order to be able to evaluate and critically discuss it.

Review	Written by someone else. If the review has been written by an expert, it may give you useful information about the context of the source and other published work in the field. However, reviews are of no use for detailed information and may often be a biased personal opinion.
Abstract	Always written by the author. Gives the outline topic and usually but not always the conclusion. You will not be able to understand each step or be able to evaluate the evidence, argument or conclusion just by reading the abstract.
Summary	Could be written by the author or by someone else. Summarises the argument and the conclusion but not in enough detail for you to be able to evaluate the evidence or argument.
Introduction and conclusion	Written by the author. These give a good idea of the main points and argument but are not enough for you to evaluate the evidence or argument.

Source selection checklist

So, before you start reading a source in detail you should be able to answer most of the following questions:

- What type of source is it?
- Who wrote it and when?
- Is it relevant, reliable and academic – and if not, is that OK?
- Is the main function of the text to describe, explain, hypothesise, argue, or some of these things together?
- Who is the text written for?
- Why are you going to read it – what exactly do you want to get out of it?
- Do you think it will generally support your conclusion or give an opposing viewpoint?

10 Write down the essentials

Keep a record of the source titles and when and how you found them. The reasons for doing this are many: to build up your personal research database, to be able to reference sources properly in your assignment and avoid accidental plagiarism, to compile reference lists and bibliographies, to show and discuss sources with your tutor, to be able to easily find the source again if you need to, to share a reference with other students and so on.

This record of sources is sometimes called a research log. You can use online software, keep a simple document file or even use index cards for your log. The important thing is that each log entry is complete. For books you must include whether the names are authors and/or editors, the edition number, the publisher and where it was published (the ISBN number is also useful). Your log should be accurate; for example, do not change the title's use of upper- or lower-case letters or punctuation.

Finally, it is useful to note down a very brief summary of the main idea, theme or position of the source. Although you may not yet have read the text in detail (and you may need to alter your entry once you have done so), by getting to the final selection stage and answering the questions in your final selection checklist, you should already have an idea of the text's general message.

Here is an example of a research log entry:

Source details:	Research details:
Oswald AJ (1997). Happiness and economic performance. *The Economic Journal* 107(445), 1815–31.	Found on 21/1/2013 by uni infolinx > e journals > JSTOR > using search phrase 'economics and happiness'.
Main idea	Also a copy in library (ref. only): JE201.2
That employment does affect happiness but less because of income and more because of the fact of having a job.	

Once you have completed all your research entries, sit back and take stock. You have now completed the first stage of your research and have your own unique collection of sources that you know are exactly right for the job.

Summary

- An excellent assignment is one that has been built properly, brick by brick. It will have a conclusion that is persuasive because it is based upon a strong argument that uses relevant and reliable evidence.

- Have the confidence to select what *you* think are the most relevant sources from your course reading list. Do this thinking for yourself first; you can then also ask your tutor for advice if you are unsure.

- The confidence to select appropriate sources comes from a clear understanding of your assignment title and from knowing what you want from each source.

- Don't be afraid to reject sources for fear that you might be missing something – there is not enough time to read everything, and at university you are expected to make such choices.

- It is *your* responsibility to check that your sources are relevant, appropriate and reliable for the type of information you need – this will usually mean using academically rigorous material.

- Use your university library.

- Keep a research log and nurture a sense of ownership of your own unique selection and collection of sources.

DECIDE *HOW* YOU ARE GOING TO READ

11 Three different ways to read

Before plunging into reading, take a few minutes to think about the best order in which to read your texts so that you keep things as motivating, interesting and time-effective as possible. For example, an effective order for reading is shown in the picture here.

START HERE

4th Sources that are older and/or less central and/or look difficult

3rd Sources that are older and/or less central

2nd Sources that are central & recent but look more difficult

1st Sources that are central to your assignment, recent & look relatively easy and/or interesting

Myth #4 You should read academic texts carefully from start to finish.

There usually isn't enough time to read everything from cover to cover, and you probably wouldn't want to anyway. We read different things in different ways. For example, we quickly scan a train timetable for specific information but we follow a recipe carefully step by step (going back to check that we have done things correctly) and we read novels from the beginning but in a relaxed way, sometimes skipping sections and even going straight to the end if we find the story boring.

For academic study you should apply the same principle that you use for anything else you read – matching the *way* you read something to *why* you are reading it. There are three different general approaches:

▸ **Scanning – looking over material quite quickly in order to pick out specific information**

For example, you might scan a library database for texts on a specific topic, or you might scan a journal article for specific information. You might also scan when you are looking back over material you have already read in order to check something.

▸ **Reading for gist – reading something fairly quickly in order to get the general idea or feel**

You might do this by reading just the headings, introduction and conclusion of a book, article or report, or you might read for gist by going over the whole text fairly quickly. You might want to read for gist in order to decide whether to reject a text or to read it in more detail. Reading for gist is also sometimes called skimming or reading for breadth.

Close reading – reading something in detail

There are a variety of reasons for reading something in detail: as background reading; as a 'way in' to a new and difficult topic; to make sure you understand a discussion of the data; or to clearly understand the steps and evidence used to put forward an argument. Close reading is also called reading for depth.

> **Attention!** It is important to remember that scanning or reading for gist is not a substitute for close reading. You *will* need to do a lot of detailed reading for academic work, and so the whole point of only scanning or gist reading some texts is to give you enough time for careful and close reading of the most important material. You therefore need to develop the skill of recognising when it is appropriate to scan, when to read for gist and when to do close, careful and reflective reading.

Ensure that the *way* you read is appropriate for *why* you are reading

In Chapter 2 we looked at different reasons to read at university:

▶ to widen your knowledge of a topic
▶ to understand a particular concept, term or model
▶ to learn about different perspectives or arguments on an issue
▶ to analyse (break down) and evaluate evidence, ideas or arguments.

By the time you settle down to read a text you should already have a good idea of why you want to read it, and this reading purpose should guide your choice of scanning, reading for gist, close reading, or using a combination of reading approaches. For example, if you want to understand the definition of a particular concept, you might just scan the text until you find where it defines it and then read just this section of the text in detail. On the other hand, if you want to analyse and evaluate a text you will need to read all or most of it in detail.

See *Studying with Dyslexia* in this series for further great reading strategies including:
• SQ3R – Survey, Question, Read, Recall and Review, p. 57.
• The Start and End technique, p. 58.
• Visual and auditory strategies, p. 63.
• Textmapping, p. 64.

Should you read on screen or on paper?

You should do whatever works best for you but here are a few points to bear in mind.

Reading on paper

Pros	Cons
• You can write, draw and highlight on the text without changing the original document.	• You have to print out, borrow or buy the text.
• You can easily flip between pages, keeping a sense of where you are in the text.	• You can't change, copy, cut, paste, convert or easily share the text.
• You can lay out and rearrange pages as you like and view them all at once to get a good idea of overall structure (textmapping).	
• You can read wherever/whenever you like without worrying about damaging or losing your device.	

Reading from the screen

Pros	Cons
• You can change, copy, cut, paste, convert and share the text in numerous ways.	• Some people find it slower to navigate through the text and find it less easy to see where they are, which can lead to a sense of feeling lost in the text.
• It might encourage you to read first and make notes from memory afterwards, making you more independent of the text.	• It can be very tempting to cut and paste different bits of a document or paste bits of different documents together and then use this edited version in assignments. This defeats the purpose of academic study and can lead to plagiarism.
• You can alter the font type, font/background colour for easier reading.	

Stay flexible

Stay flexible about which reading methods and strategies you use. You will often need to use combinations of methods, not just across different texts but also within an individual text. For example, you might first quickly read over a whole text for gist, then read a

section of it in detail, read some bits you find difficult again *very* carefully, then go back and scan the text for anything you think you may have missed. Another example of staying flexible is whether you read from the screen or paper – you might read on screen to skim some articles or to read the introduction or end of a text and then print out the texts you want to read in detail.

Review your progress as you go along

Be prepared to change your reading strategy as you go along. After reading a quarter or a third of the text, ask yourself, 'Is it giving me what I want? Am I learning and thinking as I read? Do I understand what I'm reading?'

If the answer to these questions is 'no', stop and think about why this is. It may be that you dived straight in with close reading and that it would be better to zoom out and get the general feel of the text first before going back to the detail. It may be that you need to find an easier text as a way in to the topic or perhaps that the material is not as relevant as you thought and that you should stop and move on to something else.

12 Plan the time to read

One of the main reasons why students get low marks in assignments is simply because they haven't spent enough time on all three parts of the process: reading, thinking and writing. You need to *care* about your reading, so give it a high priority.

▶ Get out of poor reading habits such as reading at times when you are rushed, tired or sleepy (reading for study just before bed is not a good idea either for reading or for sleeping!).

▶ Have both a short-term (e.g. weekly) time management plan for reading as well as a long-term one (over a semester or a whole year, including time for more relaxed background reading during holidays).

▶ Be clear to yourself and to others that you need *x* amount of time for reading and will be busy reading at *y* times. Make sure family and friends understand that reading for study is demanding, important work and not at all like reading for leisure.

▶ Find your own ideal concentration span that strikes a balance between reading for long enough to have a meaningful session and stopping before you lose concentration: for example, 30 minutes > 5 min break > another 30 mins > 5 min break > a final 30–40 mins.

▶ Mild time pressure can increase your motivation and therefore alertness, but don't put yourself under so much pressure that you rush and so don't really understand, question or reflect on what you read.

How quickly should you be reading?

There is no correct answer to this question. Understanding and thinking as you read is more important than speed, and how quickly you read a text will depend on why you are reading it. However, if you think you could do with reading a little faster, first work out roughly how quickly you read at the moment. Around 40 words per minute for an unfamiliar and difficult text and around 100+ words for an easy text is about average. You may find that your reading speed is fine as it is, but if you do want to increase your speed, try some of these techniques:

▶ Use a reading guide (e.g. a slim pointer) to keep your eyes moving forward on the page and try not to keep going back on what you have just read.

▶ Read in meaningful chunks, fixing your eyes only two or three times a line rather than slowly reading every word.

▶ If you are in the habit of vocalising the words as you read, try doing this more quickly and in your head rather than aloud.

Before you start a reading session, deal with your current distractions and worries as best you can. Writing them down and deciding what actions you will take to deal with them will help unclutter your mind.

Make sure that you have everything you need to hand, that you have adequate light (but without glare) and that the text is roughly at eye level so that you are not bending your neck.

Some people work better listening to music (research has shown that if you do, it should be quiet and soft with a faster tempo). If you are in the habit of listening to music while you study, try working for a few days without it and see if in fact you read more effectively – you may not have had to concentrate on such difficult and demanding texts before.

Summary

- Know what you want from each source before you read it.

- An effective reader is one who can match their reading strategy to their reading purpose. If you are reading everything from start to finish at the same speed, you are probably not reading efficiently.

- You need to find reading strategies that allow you to build up a 'detailed *and* broad knowledge base'.

- Be flexible and review your progress as you read to make sure that your purpose and methods remain appropriate.

- Your reading environment should balance comfort with alertness.

- You might not find everything you read very interesting but even just finding the answers to your questions and achieving your reading goal can be satisfying.

Part 4 concentrates on what you need to do in order to analyse and evaluate what a text says. This reading purpose is central to academic study and requires that you understand the text fully and accurately.

purpose – predict – scaffold – challenge – engage – enjoy

Have a quick look back at Chapter 1 on pp. 1–6 to remind yourself of these essential points for active reading.

Before you start to read in earnest you should have a general idea of the author's purpose in writing the text (an introduction to a topic? an academic discussion of ideas? presenting new research?) and why *you* want to read it. Having a clear goal in mind as you read will sharpen your focus and so increase your motivation for reading.

15 Find the key message

Let's look at features present in most types of text that can help us understand them, using two real text extracts as examples.

Extract 1 is from a report written by the Food Standards Agency (2013) titled *Front of pack food labelling: joint response to consultation.* A student found this source when working on the assignment about preventing lifestyle diseases such as coronary heart disease (see p. 22).

Below are the student's reasons for reading the report and some of their predictions and pre-reading questions, followed by the extract itself.

> *I have noticed the traffic light system of food labelling and I find this useful myself in choosing healthier food items.*

I think this report will say that labelling food with information about how/whether it contributes to a healthy diet is a good thing because it helps people make healthier choices. However, I guess that the food industry's main aim is to sell food, so it will be interesting to find out whether it supports food labelling.

What I really want to find out is what the government intends to do about food labelling and why.

I am going to read this report to see if it contains information on what the government is doing to help people eat healthily. The report might also contain some critical evaluation of preventative measures, although probably not by the people who wrote this report but by the people who were consulted.

Extract 1

Introduction

5.1 We welcome the responses to the FoP [Front of Pack] nutrition labelling consultation from a wide range of interested parties and the willingness of many organisations to work with us to achieve greater consistency for future UK FoP labelling.

5.2 Respondents have confirmed to us the importance of FoP labelling, and the need to ensure that any scheme UK Health Ministers might recommend will be one that is consistent across the food products that consumers buy and as widely applied as possible.

5.3 A range of views was expressed on the preferred format, with support for various combinations of %GDAs [guideline daily amounts], colour coding and HML text. However, post consultation, the UK's major food retailers coalesced around a hybrid scheme that includes %GDA and colour coding. An issue on which there was consensus was the need to include information on energy, fat, saturated fats, sugars and salt wherever possible. Whilst it was agreed that labelling would be most useful on composite foods, there was no consensus on the foods that should not carry FoP labelling. We therefore believe that decisions on exemptions should be made by food businesses, with the caveat that they should not set out to be misleading where they are made. In addition, given the responses to the consultation, we will work towards recommending labelling on a 'per portion' basis, and will look further at the possibility of bringing more consistency to when nutrition declarations are given 'as sold' or 'as consumed'.

5.4 Whilst it was clear that the positioning of FoP information can help consumers, prescribing a common position would not work on all packaging/product types.

5.5 There was no call for the development of a common logo and little support for guidance on the highlighting of information on energy content or other information in the form of 'pings'. Therefore, we do not intend to deliberate further on these issues.

Next Steps

5.6 UK Health Ministers announced on 24 October 2012 their desire to work towards a consistent scheme based on %GDA and colour coding. We will work with interested organisations to develop both the underlying criteria, and the presentation of a FoP label based on this approach.

5.7 Officials in all four UK countries are working towards a fully developed scheme by Spring 2013, so that industry can relabel in time to be compliant with the EU FIC.

....

Extract from: Food Standards Agency (2013) *Front of pack food labelling: joint response to consultation*, p. 30.

Use clues given in the organisation of the text

To understand the main idea or message of any text, you need to make use of the clues given in how it is organised and what the author is doing in different sections. Don't just glance over headings and subheadings – read them carefully and reflect on what they say about the author's message. Read the introduction and conclusion and the first line of each paragraph (this usually gives the key idea) to get a general idea of the author's message before drilling down to the detail. Take note of the way sections are numbered (e.g. 5.1, 5.2) as this indicates how different ideas and points have been grouped together. Finally, keep an eye out for words and phrases in bold or italics – these usually indicate key points.

Be clear on what different parts of the text are doing

You need to be able to distinguish between description, explanation, argument and opinion so that you can get a clear picture of what is going on in the text and pick out the main message.

▶ **Description**: Describes something but does *not* give reasons and does *not* try to judge or persuade the reader of something.

For example:

> Respondents have confirmed to us the importance of FoP labelling, and the need to ensure that any scheme UK Health Ministers might recommend will be one that is consistent across the food products that consumers buy and as widely applied as possible.

▶ **Explanation**: *Does* give reasons for something (and may also give a conclusion) but does *not* try to judge or persuade the reader of something.

For example:

> There was no call for the development of a common logo and little support for guidance on the highlighting of information on energy content or other information in the form of 'pings'. Therefore, we do not intend to deliberate further on these issues.

▶ **Argument**: An argument proposes a statement *and* gives reasons and evidence (these might be strong or they might be weak/illogical) that lead to a particular conclusion *and* uses these reasons and conclusion to persuade the reader of a particular idea or action.

For example:

> A range of views was expressed on the preferred format … Whilst it was agreed that labelling would be most useful on composite foods, there was no consensus on

the foods that should not carry FoP labelling. We therefore believe that decisions on exemptions should be made by food businesses, with the caveat that they should not set out to be misleading where they are made.

▸ **Opinion, agreement and disagreement**: Opinion, agreement and disagreement are points of view (perhaps but not necessarily trying to persuade) *without* supporting evidence or logical reasoning. Opinion and dis/agreement are *not* valid arguments and in an academic text should only be given in addition to a properly supported argument, not instead of one.

An example of an opinion would be: We think that consumers would prefer labelling on the back of packets rather than on the front.

Don't get distracted from the main message

Use your knowledge of the difference between background description, examples, argument and opinion to identify and separate out the main message of the argument. However, you do need to understand the argument in context, so also read the sentences before and after a key point.

Don't get distracted by side-points, examples or 'special facts' boxes put in to make the text look more interesting, and don't mistake these for the argument itself.

Use clues given in the language of a text

Let's now continue looking at the clues a text can give you by using an extract from a different source, found by a student doing the assignment on the links between a society's economic performance and levels of happiness (see p. 23).

This second extract is annotated with some of the student's pre- and post-reading thoughts, and with numbered examples of words and phrases in the text that helped the student understand it.

The extract is followed by a summary of what the numbered annotations illustrate.

Pre-reading thinking: My questions - does economic performance affect people's happiness? Why/how? My prediction - that Oswald says EP does not affect happiness.

Extract 2

Happiness and Economic Performance
Author: Andrew J. Oswald

Source: The Economic Journal, Vol. 107, No. 445 (Nov., 1997) pp. 1815-1831 Published by: Blackwell Publishing for the Royal Economic Society Stable pp 1820–1822

....

The British Household Panel Survey data show that income has no strong role to play, [in individual well-being] but that joblessness does. Clark and Oswald (1994) fail to find any statistically significant effect from income. The sharp impact of unemployment, however, is illustrated by …. data on 6,000 British workers in 1991. Mental distress is twice as high among the unemployed as among those who have work. Interestingly, research suggests that the worst thing about losing one's job is not the drop in take-home income. It is the non-pecuniary distress. To put this differently, most regression results imply that an enormous amount of extra income would be required to compensate people for having no work.

① Important verb used to state the main argument

② Emphasises the contrast between the point made in this sentence and the previous one

③ Word to look up now

④ Rephrasing a point

⑤ Word to look up later

Table 5 *The Microeconomics of Happiness in Europe: 1975–86*

	All	Unemployed
Very happy (%)	23.4	15.9
Pretty happy (%)	57.9	51.1
Not too happy (%)	18.6	33.0
	Lowest income quartile people	Highest-income quartile people
Very happy (%)	18.8	28.4
Pretty happy (%)	54.5	58.5
Not too happy (%)	26.7	13.1

Source: Di Tella et al. (1996) using Eurobarometer data.
Total sample 108,802 observations.

⑥ All people in the sample of 108,802 compared with only the unemployed people in the same sample.

⑦ Less than a fifth of the <u>whole sample</u> were 'not too happy' but less than a third of the <u>unemployed people</u> in the sample were 'not too happy'.

⑦ Double the number of people on low income were 'not too happy' compared to the people on a high income.

⑧ You will find the full details of primary sources in the list of references. Note that the research was conducted over 14 years ago.

Post-reading thinking: Do the statistics about people on low and high income support Oswald's argument? How does this data compare with today?

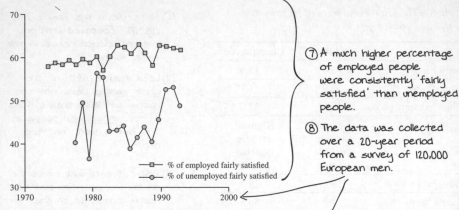

Fig. 1 Life-satisfaction levels of the employed and the unemployed: the European countries 1970s–1990s. *Notes.* The vertical axis measures the proportion of people saying they were 'fairly satisfied with life' as a whole. The data source is the Eurobarometer Surveys, which provide a random sample here of approximately 120,000 European men. Running a trend line through each series produces almost exactly the same gradient, namely, just over 0.2.

<u>Post-reading thinking</u>: There was a very sharp fall in happiness in unemployed <u>men</u> in the late 1970s followed by a very sharp rise in the early 1980s – how might this be explained? Would women have followed a similar pattern?

Eurobarometer data, in Table 5 and Fig. 1, also show that the unemployed feel much less satisfied with life,[6] and indicate that the relative distress from unemployment does not appear to be trending downwards through the years (the 'unhappiness gap' is not secularly shrinking). In passing this might be thought to raise doubts about the oft-expressed view that an increasingly generous welfare state is somehow at the root of Europe's economic problems. A review of psychologists' earlier work is available in Warr et al. (1988). The upshot of all this evidence is:

FINDING 3. Unemployed people are very unhappy.

(Conclusion page 1828)
The conclusions of the paper do not mean that economic forces have little impact on people's lives. A consistent theme through the paper's different forms of evidence has been the vulnerability of human beings to joblessness. Unemployment appears to be the ordinary economic source of unhappiness. If so, economic growth should not be a government's primary concern.

<u>Post-reading thinking - evaluation after reading the article:</u> Expert author, persuasive argument - worth reading. But some of the evidence is perhaps selective and Oswald makes generalisations? I need to find further evidence from other sources.

(Margin annotations:)

9 — These verbs link to 'data'

10 — Indicates a side point

11 — Refers to the fact that the 'unhappiness gap' is not shrinking

12 — Important word for understanding the context of the argument accurately

Summary of annotations

①	Verbs that show what the author thinks	⑦	Data – what is shown – key statistics
②	Linking/contrasting words	⑧	Data – who collected it, when and where
③	Words you need to know to understand the text	⑨	Understanding what verbs in the sentence refer to
④	Phrases that indicate rephrasing of a point	⑩	Phrases that indicate *minor* points
⑤	Words you can look up after reading	⑪	Checking what words such as *this/ that* refer to
⑥	Data – what is measured	⑫	Words that are important for accurate understanding of the argument

Three useful types of language clue

1 Look out for language 'signposts' which tell you that a main point, change or section is coming up (NB: Oswald does not use many signposts as his writing style is very direct).

For example:
There are three main problems … First, … second … finally …
The question/issue/point is …

The main cause/effect/result/effect/implication/flaw is ...
Importantly, ...
My argument is that ...
The conclusion is ...

The author might also use language signposts to indicate that s/he is repeating or rephrasing an important point. For example: *to put this differently / in other words / so / another way of saying this is ...*

2 Look at the verbs the author uses, as these give important clues to what they are doing:

For example:

suggest/propose/imply	setting out their argument
illustrate/indicate/ prove/show/ establish/demonstrate	giving supporting evidence and/or main points
question/query/challenge/dispute/reject	disagreeing with someone else
fail to/claim	*about* to disagree with someone else

3 Be aware of how authors use words such as *may/might/possibly/tends to* to indicate how sure or unsure they are about their claim or how strong or weak they think a correlation is:

For example:

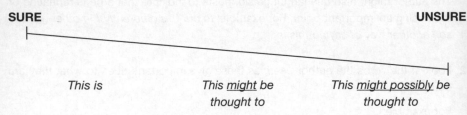

SURE   **UNSURE**

This is   *This might be*   *This might possibly be*
                              thought to   *thought to*

Make sure you have understood *accurately*

✅ 'Sources used accurately and concisely ...'

❌ '... inaccurate reading and limited understanding ...'

Understanding and communicating precisely is crucial in all academic work. A very common mistake in reading is to misunderstand what a text says because you have not understood fully and accurately. Common student pitfalls include:

▶ misinterpreting the main point of the data

Take a few minutes to try to understand the overall key message of the data rather than getting bogged down in the details. Once you have understood the point the author is trying to make with the data you can go back and analyse it in detail.

▶ misinterpreting or not noticing comparatives or superlatives such as *better / the best / worse / the worst / greater / the greatest*

For example, Oswald does not say that the distress of not having a job is just one of the negative things about losing one's job but that it is *the worst* thing.

▶ not accurately understanding the degree of something

For example, Oswald does not only state that unemployed people are less satisfied with life but that they are *much* less satisfied.

Similarly, it would be wrong to say that Oswald states that economic forces have a huge impact on happiness. Oswald does not in fact say how much economic forces affect happiness, just that they do have an effect.

▶ overlooking the words *not* or *no*

Pay careful attention to *not*, *no* and other phrases that indicate a negative – mistakes here mean that you might accidentally reverse the author's meaning.

For example:

'Clark and Oswald (1994) *fail to* find …'

'The conclusions of this paper do *not* mean that economic forces …'

▶ misinterpreting who says what

For example, it would be incorrect to say that Oswald's findings show that income does not significantly affect happiness – this finding came from different research conducted by Clark and Oswald.

If you are not sure whether you have understood a text accurately, check with your tutor or other students on your course.

✅ '... willingness to engage critically with the literature and ability to go beyond it ...'

❌ '... does not go beyond the assertion of points derived from the literature'

✅ '... ability to analyse materials and their implications'

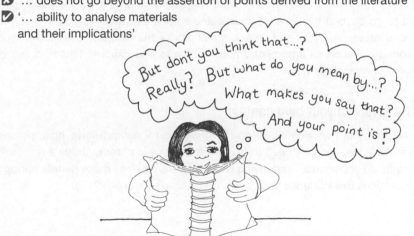

Critical thinking

Myth #5 There is only one correct way to understand a text.

Myth #6 You can't really disagree with an academic text because you are not an expert in that subject.

Although you need to understand what the author is saying on the page, you also need to go beyond this level of understanding and decide what *you* think about the author's message. You need to ask questions of the text and then form your own reasoned views on its argument, importance and implications. This is called *critical thinking* or *critical analysis*.[1]

1 Be aware of your own context

We all bring our own context to anything we read – our individual bias, perspective and experience – and we need to be aware of these in order to judge a text fairly. For example, do you have an underlying belief that wealth *does* make people happy and if so, how does this influence your views on Oswald's argument?

---

[1] See *Getting Critical,* 2nd edn, in this series.

2 Be aware of the author's context

Authors are human beings and so will also have their own context. Find out who the author is and who they work for (the 'about us' sections on websites, Google and Wikipedia are useful sources of information). Find out what historical, political and social context they are/were writing in and whether they have a particular ideological stance (e.g. Marxist, conservative, feminist). How might these contexts affect what the author hoped to achieve?

Also be aware of the context of reports and other commissioned documents. For example, the report on front-of-pack food labelling has been written on behalf of the Food Standards Agency. This is a non-ministerial government body whose board is appointed by the Secretary of State for Health, and board members include people who have a background in food production, PR and marketing.

3 Challenge the author and identify assumptions, gaps and flaws

As you read (perhaps at a second reading), engage the author in a conversation in your mind and challenge them. Remember that thinking critically does not mean that you *have* to disagree with what they say – you might disagree or you might agree. You also do need to try to understand the author's point of view before you can challenge it.

- What assumptions is the author's argument based on and do you think these are correct? For example, one main underlying assumption in the Oswald text extract (as apparent from the conclusion) is that it is the government's role to decrease unemployment.

- Look at the author's use of evidence. Do their reasons and conclusion link together logically or are there gaps or flaws in the argument?
  For example, does the data in Table 5 on p. 75 really support Oswald's argument? Also, Oswald claims that 'Unemployed people are very unhappy' yet the data on which Oswald bases this claim is collected from men only (read the small print under Fig.1 on p. 76).

- The way in which data and other research is used is important. Check who the research team of a paper work for. Is their bibliography correct and are they aware of other current research in the field? Have proper controls and error analyses been conducted? Could there be other explanations for their correlations and conclusions? Could they have done things in a more efficient way? If primary data has been used in a secondary source, has it been reported and used fairly?

▶ Be aware of opinion, agreement or disagreement that is not supported by evidence and reasoning. Phrases such as *surely/we have to remember/it is perfectly clear that/it is obvious that/it is a fact that/one can't fail to recognise that* are sometimes used to persuade the reader that something is true without providing any actual evidence. Emotive phrases such as *completely/absolutely/merely/hardly/only* are also sometimes used as 'empty persuaders'.

4 Evaluate

After your critical analysis, stand back, reflect and give the text a final evaluation. What is the way of thinking of the author? What is the text trying to do and how well does it do it? Why do you think people read this text? Do *you* think it is worth reading and why?

- ✔ '... mindful of other interpretations ...'
- ✔ '... clear understanding of the nature of the material'
- ✘ '... lack of awareness of the context of the material'

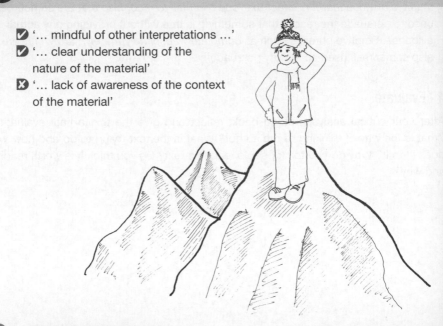

Location, location, location!

After reflecting on the specific text you have read, relate it to the other material you have read on that topic. As you read more, you need to build up a mental picture of the 'location' of different authors. How do the texts differ and how are they similar? Where does each author 'sit' in the subject? Which authors agree with each other and which disagree? Are there any authors who are 'out there' with their own novel idea? Who are the Old Masters and who are the emerging stars?

Develop your understanding

Don't underestimate the importance of discussing your reading and ideas with other students and with your tutors. Make the most of seminars and study groups, and use reference lists and bibliographies from key texts to find relevant further reading. Discussing different angles and interpretations is a key part of understanding the context and nature of your material – the wider picture.

Myth #7 If you don't understand something or feel confused, it is probably because you are being a bit thick.

Feeling confused?

Reading means learning new things, and feeling a bit nervous and confused can in fact be a sign that your brain is absorbing, learning and fitting in the new information with the old – a good and normal process! New learning and understanding takes time. Even professors find some texts difficult and have to re-read them, look up words they don't know and use other techniques to help them get to grips with new material.

▶ Brainstorm on the topic and relate it to what you already know before you start reading in order to activate the relevant scaffold in your brain.

▶ If you are getting stuck or find yourself reading the same sentence over and over again, have a break and then write a short summary or reflection on what you have read so far. This will help your brain assimilate the new information and when you go back to your reading, you will usually discover that you now understand more clearly.

Difficult text?

Myth #8 Intelligent people and good readers usually only need to read things once.

If you feel (or have been told) that you are not a great reader, this is probably due to lack of experience, practice and good reading strategies rather than a lack of intelligence. If you find yourself struggling with a difficult text, it could also be because the chapter or article you are reading is poorly written!

- Remember the process of purpose > motivation > understanding. Not having a clear purpose can make you feel anxious and restless and easily distracted by familiar things such as housework or watching TV.

- If you are losing motivation, remind yourself of your initial reasons for choosing the text, module and even course.

- If the text is complex and dense, find an easier way in, such as zooming out before going back to the detail, reading simpler texts on the topic or discussing the text with a colleague or tutor.

- If you really have tried but just can't understand a particular text, try not to feel stressed about it and just move on to a different one.

Dealing with words you don't understand

Myth #9 You should look up all the words you don't understand as you go along.

Don't look up every unknown word as you read as this will slow you down and break your concentration. Look up the words you think you need to understand the text and just underline the others to look up later (but do look them up).

There is no magic pill for developing your word knowledge, and exhaustive research has shown that we learn new words over time by – you guessed it – reading. However, for academic study you will need to speed up your vocabulary development, and there are several things you can do to achieve this:

- Don't just learn the word on the page. To be able to actively use a word you need to know its other forms (e.g. noun, adjective, verb, negative) and which words are always or usually used before and after it (e.g. in/at/on).
- Buy and *use* a good dictionary and read through the guide at the front. A good dictionary will give you most of the information you need to be able to use a word properly.
- Make a note of useful words and phrases that keep coming up and practise using them precisely. A common student error is to use words in a nearly but not quite right way. See *The Student Phrase Book* (Godfrey 2013) for useful academic vocabulary.

Dealing with sentences you don't understand

Academic texts should be written in a clear style although you will often come across complex sentences that have several different parts such as this one!

Tips for unpacking a difficult sentence:

1 Break it down into its separate parts. Sentences are usually divided by commas or semi-colons or words such as *and/or/but/although/which/that/such as*. Our example sentence given above can be broken down into four parts:

> Academic texts should be written in a clear style
>
> although you will often come across complex sentences
>
> that have several different parts
>
> such as this one.

2 Find the subjects and verbs in the sentence that go together.

3 Check that you are clear on the meaning of words that *link* sentences or parts of a sentence

> E.g. *however/nevertheless/despite/although/whereas/moreover/ also/in addition.*

4 Be clear about what words such as *it/these/they/this/this one/which/that/such* are referring to.

5 Read the sentences before and after the problematic one.

6 Write out the sentence in your own words.

Summary

▶ Have the confidence to know that your course reading *will* get easier with practice and time.

▶ If you are finding a text difficult, recognise your feelings, accept that they are normal and then use specific strategies to move forward, including having a break or moving on to a different text.

▶ Make sure you are clear on the function and structure of the whole text and of its different parts so that you can clearly separate out the key information or argument.

▶ You need to understand the words on the page, and your vocabulary will not develop by magic – you need to be proactive and note down, learn and use words and phrases that are new to you.

▶ Develop a critical approach in order to come to your own reasoned views about the author's message.

▶ Understanding different author objectives and identifying the similarities and differences between different texts is the final step in really grasping the nature of your reading material.

Making notes

19 Why bother making notes?

In Part 1 we looked at how university study requires active learning, and how making any type of notes will help you to activate your thought processes. In terms of making notes from reading, the mental and physical activity of noting down thoughts and questions **before you read**, making some notes **while you read** (although you may prefer not to take any notes while reading) and then adding further notes, comments and reflections **when you have finished reading** will all help you to engage critically with the texts.

Have a clear purpose

As we saw in Chapters 2 and 3, to be effective your notes need to be *purposeful* and *meaningful*. A clear purpose is just as important for note making as it is for reading

– your notes should address the questions you want answered. Think also about the function you want your notes to fulfil. For example, do you want your notes to:

- extract all the essential points and arguments?
- note down only information on a specific theme?
- focus only on information that addresses your own angle or question?
- find further references?
- clarify how the points relate to each other and see how the ideas are organised?
- reorganise or connect the information in a new way?
- develop your own thoughts and argument on the issue?

Advantages of making notes

You make notes for yourself, not for anybody else, and they can take any form, including diagrams, pictures or speech rather than writing (see Chapters 23 and 24). Regardless of how you create notes on what you read, the act of making them will:

- help you to concentrate on what you are reading
- keep you motivated by tracking and signalling your progress
- help you remember information more easily
- start you on the process of using your own words and style
- give you your own unique record of the text

- help you to reflect and make connections between different pieces of knowledge, leading to a better understanding of your subject
- save you time when it comes to writing your assignment
- probably result in higher marks.

> **Warning!** There are a couple of things to watch out for when making notes.
>
> Firstly, just copying down points can give you the *illusion* of doing something active when in fact you are not really doing anything useful.
>
> Secondly, if you don't record carefully the difference between sections of your notes that are words or information copied from the text and those bits that are your own words and thoughts, when you come to use your notes in an assignment you might accidentally either plagiarise or attribute views to the source that are in fact your own. The next couple of chapters will give you tips on avoiding both of these pitfalls.

Whatever the purpose of your notes and whatever form they take, they should make sense to you and be fairly brief while still providing you with an accurate, clear and complete picture.

You will often want your notes to help you critically evaluate what you are reading and so, before you start, think about what *you* feel are the main issues and what *you* think about the topic. Even if you know very little about the topic, you should still try to come up with your own questions and initial viewpoint, as this will provide you with a platform from which to critically evaluate the text.

Key feature	Why?
Full reference details (similar to a research log entry) and the relevant page numbers	You will only be able to use your notes in your assignment if you can give full reference details. Reference details will also help you find sources if you need to check back. Make sure you note down when the author of the text cites *other* authors.
Information on when/where you made the notes	This will help you recall associations and trains of thought later.
Your purpose and questions written at the top of your notes	This will keep your notes focused and help stop you from taking notes that you don't need and will never use. If you are worried about needing information at a later date, just write down a key word/phrase and then you can use your research log to find the details later if you need to.
Information that is not too detailed or too brief	If your notes are too brief, the meaning will be unclear and you won't understand them in a month's or year's time. If your notes are too detailed then it probably means you are copying from the text – note making does not mean copying whole sections from the text.

Key feature	Why?
Clear distinction between the main points/argument and minor points/examples	If you find you can't separate out the main points, it means that you don't really understand the text. Think about whether you even need to make notes on minor points.
Meaningful use of abbreviations	Using abbreviations will help prevent copying and will encourage you to use your own style. Keep a record of what key abbreviations mean.
A clear system for distinguishing between:	
exact phrases from the text (quotations)	You must keep careful track of quotations (even very short ones) in your notes to make sure that you reference them in your final assignment – use colour, quotation marks or write them in a separate space.
mostly **the same words from the text, or a mixture of your words and those from the text (close paraphrase)**	Again, keep a careful track of this – for your assignment you will need to rewrite these bits so that they are completely or almost completely (90%) in your own words.

Key feature	Why?
your *own* words to describe information from the text (paraphrase)	Do try to use your own words and style as much as possible. You may be worried about changing the meaning of the text, of 'moving away' from it, or feel that you can't put things into your own words as well as the original. However, using at least some of your own words in your notes will help you to start the paraphrasing process. Your confidence will increase with practice.
your own comments and ideas	It's a good idea to have a separate column or space for these.
White space	In case you need to add anything later.

Read first, note later

Try reading the text first *without* making any notes and then summarise it in your mind or out loud. Make notes without looking back at the text and then go back to it if you need to check anything.

Go easy on the highlighter

If you really do want to mark the text at a first reading, just pick out the most relevant sections by putting a line down alongside them, using a pencil rather than a high-lighter. You probably won't really get a clear idea of the key points of a text until you have got to the end; therefore if you highlight as you read for the first time, you may be stuck with highlighting that you later want to change. A better use of the highlighter might be to use it on your notes for bringing out key points.

Do more than just annotate

Annotating a text is fine, but also try to write notes that are separate from the text. Online note-making software usually only allows you to make short annotations on or around the text and so, again, also make your own notes either on a separate e-document or on paper.

Explain your reactions to yourself

It's good to react to the text, but don't just put **!!** or **?** in the margin – write out clearly and precisely what your thoughts are.

Avoid secretary syndrome

Myth #10 Good notes should have all the points from the text copied down.

You should *make* notes, not *take* notes. Unless you are trying to learn something by heart, there isn't much point in copying down lots of individual sentences or chunks from the text; this usually means that you are on auto pilot rather than actively reading and thinking. Try to build up the confidence to read and think first and then make notes in your own words that address your own questions. Only copy down phrases as quotations if they are really special and powerful.

Avoid secretary syndrome

Write short summary comments

As you make notes, write short summaries in your own words. Your choice of verbs in these summaries should accurately reflect what the author is doing in the text. In the summary of notes on p. 110, for example, the student writes: 'The report *states* that respondents want a food labelling system but *proposes* that the exemptions to such a system are decided by the food manufacturers.

More top tips

▸ Do some preparation. Write down what you predict the text will say, what your main questions of the text are, why you are going to make notes and what you want to produce from them later.

▸ Read or listen once without making notes.

▸ At the top of your notes put the source title and a key to particular abbreviations you are going to use.

▸ Number each page and at the top of each page write down your main purpose, question and source title – this will keep you focused and identify the pages and source if you drop or mix up your notes.

▸ Use only one side of paper: this will allow you to see all your notes at once when you come to review them.

▸ Don't try to write too quickly or try to fit too much on to one page or you may end up with notes you can't read later.

▸ Start notes for a new text on a new page. This will allow you to separate out notes on different sources when you come to review and reorganise them.

▸ *Don't* cut and paste or copy sections from your source texts as this can easily lead to accidental plagiarism.

▸ Try to review your notes within 24 hours of making them (see Part 7).

Here's an example of some good linear notes from the text extract on **pp. 68–9**. Notice that the student has not copied down any quotations but has used mainly their own words. They have also used a separate column for their own comments and thoughts, which makes clear which points are information from the report and which are the student's own ideas.

1

Food Standards Agency (Jan. 2013). *Front of pack food labelling: joint response to consultation*

Policy paper by Department of Health.

https://www.gov.uk/government/publications/response-to-consultation-on-front-of-pack-nutrition-labelling--2

Accessed, read and notes made on 13/12/2013. Found by searching on the FSA homepage.

For 'reports on food labelling'.

My purpose and Qs:

To find out what govt. is doing re food labelling and health (esp. CHD) and to see if the report has any critical evaluation or comments from the people it consulted.

My prediction – this govt. report will be biased towards the food industry who I guess won't want food labelling on unhealthy foods as this might reduce sales.

My comments/questions	Notes on text
	p. 30:
What does 'wide range' mean? Me to look at back of report to find out who was consulted.	5.1. A wide range of interested parties were consulted.
	5.2. Respnds. want any govt. scheme to be consistent and widely applicable.
How was feedback received after the consultation??	5.3. After consultation the main view was ('coalesced') for a scheme that combined %GDA with colour coding. All agreed that labels should include info. on 'energy, fat, saturated fat, sugars and salt'.
What does this comb. mean in practice? Won't a comb. be confusing?	
Key point	**Respnds. said that most useful labelling would be for 'composite' foods but couldn't agree on what should not be labelled ∴ the report recs. that exceptions should be decided on by the food industry, as long as it isn't 'misleading'.**
Exceptions to be chosen by manufs. contradicts the idea of consistency above. This seems to me to be a fudge in favour of the manufs.	
Who/how is 'misleading' decided on?	Govt. will also try to progress 'per portion' and 'as sold' or 'as consumed' info. on labelling.
<u>I need to read other bits of report to find out what this means exactly.</u>	5.4. Having the info. in same position on all packaging won't work. No support for having a common logo or catch phrases.
Has this been done?	Promised actions: a consistent scheme that combines %GDAs and colour coding by Spring 2013.
<u>Me to research further.</u>	

> **My summary and viewpoint**
> The report states that respondents want a food labelling system but proposes that the exemptions to such a system are decided by the food manufacturers.
>
> This Dept. of Health report shows progress on food labelling and a specific target for Spring 2013 to bring UK in line with EU regulations on clear food labelling. However, I think that using a combination of %GDA and colour coding is unnecessarily and purposely confusing for consumers (previous report Lobstein et al. showed that consumers prefer the colour traffic lights system). Also, allowing the food industry to choose when and when not to label foods definitely seems to be a cynical attempt to favour sales over consumers' health.

Below is a second example of some effective notes, this time pattern notes on the extract from the Oswald article on pp. 74–7. Notice that the student has only copied down one sentence and that they have marked this by putting it in quotation marks.

Oswald AJ (1997) Happiness and Economic Performance.
The Economic Journal 107 (445), p1815–31.   Found from Infolinx → ejournals → JSTOR.
Notes – pp 1815 & 1828. Made on 17/11/2013

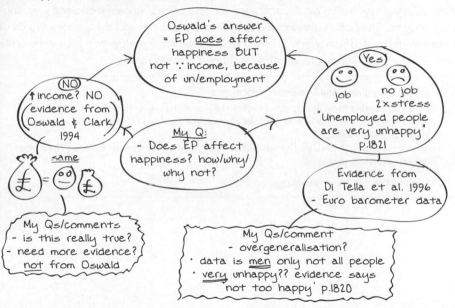

An example of some poor notes

Here are some linear notes on the Oswald extract that are not so good. They don't have adequate reference details and are a mixture of copied sentences and meaningless phrases. They don't distinguish between the student's and the author's words or between major and minor points. They lack space for the student's own comments and – worst of all – do not record the main point Oswald makes.

> Oswald A.J. **Happiness and Economic Performance**.
> – British Household Panel survey data show that income has no strong role to play.
> – mental stress is twice as high among the unemployed as among those who have work.
> – the gap is not shrinking.
> – raises doubts about the view that an increasingly generous welfare state is at the root of Europe's economic problems.
>
> **Unemployed people are very unhappy.**

Summary

- Going straight from reading to writing your assignment without making any notes bypasses key elements in the critical thinking process and makes it harder to develop and express your own independent understanding of the topic.

- Active note making means having a 'before, during and after' approach:
  - thinking about *why* you want to make notes and what you want at the end of it
  - selecting appropriate information as you (re)read and make notes
  - using your own words where possible and recording when you have copied from the text
  - adding your own questions, ideas and comments
  - reviewing, summarising and reworking your notes.

- Notes do not have to be particularly neat – you are writing them for yourself – but you do need to be able to read and understand them in a few weeks', months' or even years' time.

MATCH YOUR METHOD TO YOUR CONTEXT

Different note-making formats

You probably already use a particular note-making style but you might find it useful to spend a little time experimenting with one or two different formats. Remember also that it is sometimes a good idea to vary your note-making style according to your purpose, the subject matter and the type of material from which you are making notes (book, video, lecture, podcast etc.).

Below is a list of the main note-making formats with key points and short examples. However, remember that you make notes for yourself, not anybody else, so don't feel that you have to stick to these formats or indeed use just one format throughout your notes – mix and match in whatever way works for you.

Linear or list notes

Linear notes are notes written out in lines, often using lists, bullet points and numbering. They are an easy format to type and are good for distinguishing between major and minor points and examples. Linear notes are handy if the information is fairly ordered and has steps, stages or groupings. It's a good idea to start each new point on a new line and to use indentation and spacing to show how information groups together.

Don't forget to leave white space somewhere on the page for adding things later.

> 4 main pieces of evidence that econ. progress =
>   only v small ↗ in happiness:
> Reported happiness in US - only fractional ↗
>   post-war.
> Europe - only slightly higher levels than 20 yrs
>   ago.

Cornell or 'split page' notes

This means making linear-style notes and leaving a left-hand column for your own comments and ideas, plus a space for your own summary at the bottom. Use spacing to separate out different points or sections or topics.

The notes on p.109 are an example of this split-page format.

Paragraph notes

This is when you read/listen without making notes and then write your own summary afterwards in the form of a paragraph. This is good for expressing the key points of the information in your own words and for helping you to process and understand the text (you also often need to write a summary paragraph when you explain, share or discuss something online). One disadvantage of summary paragraph notes is that you probably won't be able to remember large amounts or details of information.

> Oswald gives four pieces of evidence to support his claim that economic progress has increased happiness only very slightly. First, happiness has only gone up a tiny bit in developed countries since the Second World War; second, Europe has only slightly higher happiness levels compared to 20 years ago; third
> ...

Pattern, visual and nuclear notes

This is when you use patterns, visual maps, spidergrams etc. to make notes. Pattern notes can help you remember information and are good for noting down the overall structure of someone's argument and for seeing connections between things. Pattern (also called visual) notes often have the key idea in the middle with other information branching off and so are also sometimes called nuclear notes.

If you use pattern notes, make sure that they still have the essential features listed on p. 101–3, for example the source and page numbers and a system to distinguish between your own words and those copied from the text.

The example notes on p. 111 are in a visual, nuclear format.

Flowcharts

Notes in the form of a flowchart are useful if the text involves sequences and processes.

Mind maps

These are like nuclear or pattern notes but are usually made before or after other forms of note making. Mind maps are used to brainstorm your *own* ideas and thoughts either before you read or to help see connections between sources after reading. Mind maps are also commonly used to brainstorm content and structure for an assignment.

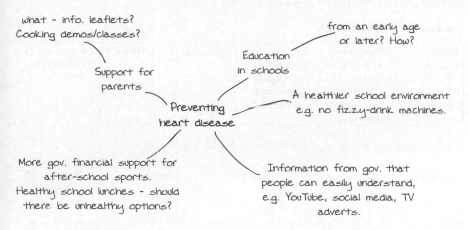

what – info. leaflets?
Cooking demos/classes?

Support for parents

from an early age or later? How?

Education in schools

Preventing heart disease

A healthier school environment e.g. no fizzy-drink machines.

More gov. financial support for after-school sports.
Healthy school lunches – should there be unhealthy options?

Information from gov. that people can easily understand, e.g. YouTube, social media, TV adverts.

Table notes

Using tables can be useful for topics and information that have several different strands or similar aspects that you want to compare, for looking at two sides of an argument, and for noting the advantages and disadvantages of something. For example, you might want to use a table to note different authors' ideas on the same topic or different student viewpoints in preparation for a debate.

Theories of job satisfaction

Affect	Dispositional	Equity	Discrepancy	2 factor	Job characteristics
Edwin A. Locke. Most famous theory. ...	Judge, Locke, Durham, Staw. Innate dispositions that ...	Idea that people are concerned mainly with ...			

You can also use tables to make a framework for your notes:

Key point	Evidence	Example	References	Own Qs & thoughts

Different note-making formats to exploit your learning style

People vary in their preferred ways of learning. Some of us learn more effectively using visual prompts, some by writing things down, some by hearing something … and most of us use a mixture of these different learning mediums.

Below is a list of note-making styles, formats and ideas grouped under different learning mediums, based on Neil Fleming's 2006 VARK model of learning styles. You might like to think about how you learn best and experiment with some of the suggestions below.

Formats for a visual (seeing) learning style:

▶ highlighters, colour coding, different sizes and styles of fonts, underlining
▶ charts, graphs and flow charts instead of tables and lists
▶ mind maps
▶ convert words into diagrams and symbols; use circles and boxes
▶ word pictures: use pictures to show ideas and represent words pictorially; use picture flash cards
▶ arrange words into patterns on the page: scattered text with white spaces/blank areas.

Formats for an aural (listening) learning style:

- listen to podcasts of lectures
- record: verbally record notes and your own thoughts and summaries and play back.

Formats for a read/write learning style:

- linear notes, and use numbering, lettering and lists: a, b, c or i, ii, iii, etc.
- bullet points and hierarchies to show priority and order
- headings, subheadings and 'wordy' mind maps
- keywords: mnemonics; glossaries; acronyms
- rewrite ideas and principles in your own words.

24 Making notes from lectures and audio-visual material

Face-to-face lectures

It can be difficult to listen and/or watch a lecture and simultaneously make notes. Listening to a face-to-face lecture is hard because you have no control over speed and can't go back or continually ask the speaker to repeat something (some lectures are easier to understand than others!).

However, you should not let these difficulties cause you to skip lectures; they are highly valuable to your studies and you should make the most of them. While lectures do not on their own make up your course, they do give you a structure and spring-board from which to learn and think about your subject. Understanding your lectures and making meaningful notes from them will get easier with practice.

Online lectures and other audio-visual material

With online lectures, podcasts, videos, DVDs etc. you can play, pause and replay the material. What you need to be careful of here is spending too much time repeatedly viewing the material and getting bogged down in detailed notes, rather than understanding the main message and seeing the wider picture.

Strategies and tips

Most of the note-making tips, strategies and features we looked at in Part 5 apply also to making notes from audio and visual material, particularly the importance of thinking about things **before**, **during** and **after**. For face-to-face lectures, doing the 'before' and 'after' work is important because of the restrictions of real-time listening, and when viewing audio-visual material you still need to make sure you prepare and follow up so that you get the most out of viewing once or twice rather than five or six times.

Below is a list of strategies and tips that will help you make the most of lectures and viewed material.

BEFORE

- Do the reading or other preparation your tutor/lecturer asks you to do.
- Make sure you understand key terms and vocabulary – this will make a huge difference to how much you understand during the lecture/material.
- Check the module website regularly (including the day before the lecture) in case the lecturer has posted any last-minute changes, additional information or guidance.
- Brainstorm what you already know about the topic, how it relates to past lectures and material (browse through past lecture handouts and notes) and what your questions and ideas about it are – jot down some notes.
- Read any handouts or slides if available (you can apply reading techniques such as Survey, Question, Read, Recall and Review – SQ3R – to lecture handouts and slides). You may like to download and print lecture PowerPoint (PPt) slides beforehand so that you can make notes on them during the lecture. (Alternatively, you can open the PPt slides and make notes during the lecture – see below.)
- Prepare a note-making framework or table.

DURING

- For face-to-face lectures, arrive on time and have the right note-making materials ready. Sit towards the front of the lecture room – it's very easy to become disengaged if you are sitting at the back. If you have no choice but to sit further back, be aware that you will need to make a real effort to stay focused and not get distracted by other students.

- Different lecturers have different lecturing styles, so familiarise yourself with each lecturer's style, their pace and how they convey ideas so that you can adapt your note making to their different styles.

- If the lecturer gives a handout at the start of a face-to-face lecture, you can make notes on this as you go along, but *don't* try to read it while the lecturer is speaking; prioritise listening and save reading the handout till afterwards.

- Leave a large margin of white space on your notepad so that you can correct and add things after the lecture.

- The lecturer will often start by outlining the structure of the content to come and the key points s/he will discuss, so *listen* to this without making any notes.

- Listen out for signpost language that will help you understand the structure, direction and key points of the lecture. For example:

Structure and logical sequence:

first, second, third, next, then, there are three main consequently, because of this, for this reason, as a result, this is due to, therefore, one effect is

Cue words for important points:

Crucially, importantly, remember, especially, obviously, as I said before

Words that qualify a statement:

always, sometimes, usually, generally, rarely, never, only

Cue words for a change in direction or contrast:

in contrast, on the other hand, a different, but, however, although

Words that indicate examples or supporting evidence:

such as, for example, for instance, an illustration of this is, research/a study by x shows that, evidence from y shows that

Making notes from lectures and audio-visual material

- As you listen to the lecture, *don't* try to write everything down – you need to leave time to really listen and understand what the lecturer is saying and capture the main messages. Just make notes on the key points and briefly jot down your own comments and questions.
- Listen out for when the lecturer emphasises important points by raising their voice or by speaking more slowly and repeating key messages. They may also use body language to emphasise points.
- It's not enough to listen – you need to listen *carefully* and to understand what the lecturer is saying *fully* and *accurately*, just as for a written text. For example, you need to be clear about whether the lecturer is giving a fact, description, explanation, example, argument or opinion. You also need to listen out for words that qualify a statement (e.g. *always*, *rarely*) or for words that negate such as *no* or *not* (see pp. 81–2).
- Listen for breaks between topics and also at the end of the lecture, when the lecturer might summarise the most important points covered.
- If the lecturer refers to a source, note this down and find the full reference as soon as possible after the lecture (ask the lecturer to write the author's name on the board if necessary).

- If you have access to the PPt slides before the lecture, you can open them and make notes during the lecture in the *notes page* box under each slide (squash up each slide by moving up its bottom edge so that you have more room in the notes box.)

Key points on student vocabulary acquisition
1 How many words do L2 students need to know?
2 Do students learn vocabulary through incidental reading, focused teaching, reading strategies and guessing?
3 Importance of learning phrases rather than isolated words?
4 Core academic vocabulary versus discipline-specific?
5 Need for practice and precision?

---

1. NNSs: Rundell – about 7500 words above basic 2–3000 threshold level to understand 92–93% of a serious text. Nation – 8000 words = 97–98% coverage of serious newspapers. 9000 are needed for 98% coverage. Size of lexicon needed for native-speaker performance – about 17,000–20,000 word families.

2. Incidental reading is good but focused teaching is also needed. Teaching vocabulary is more useful than focusing on reading strategies (Dalton et al., Haynes and Baker, Laufer). Trying to guess words definitely doesn't work (Bensoussan and Laufer, Laufer 1997).

3. High. (Nattinger and De Carrico, Kilgarrif, ? ? Nesselhauf and others.)

4. Both are important. (Durrant et al., Corson, Coxhead, Hyland and ?)

5. Definitely. Established pedagogy.

- In a face-to-face lecture you can ask the lecturer to repeat or clarify something – they often don't mind and if they say no, you haven't lost anything.
- Remember that you don't have to make notes. You might find it more useful to prepare well beforehand, listen carefully to the lecture and then make some notes (including your own comments and questions) immediately after the lecture.
- If you can't or don't want to make notes during a lecture, record it and listen to it later. Always ask the lecturer for permission to record.

AFTER

- You need to become a *critical* listener – that is, to ask questions and evaluate for yourself what you have heard or seen. However, it is not always possible to listen/watch and to be critical at the same time, so critically reviewing the lecture or material as soon as possible afterwards is important.
- Analyse the lecture/material content and write down your own evaluation, ideas and questions. What follow-up questions would you like to ask? What further research and references do you want to chase up? How does the content relate to the rest of the module and your course in general? What really interested you?
- Review and amend your notes if necessary to make sure that you can understand them and that they make sense. Underline key points, correct any errors, fill in points you missed and look up any words or terms you don't understand.

- If you used the notes pages to add notes to a PPt lecture, you can review the presentation and delete any less important or irrelevant slides. You can then print out the slides and your notes by going to *Print* and selecting *Notes view* on the *Print what?* menu.
- If you have recorded a lecture, listen to it again as soon as possible and make notes and/or fill in any important gaps.
- Using your notes, write a short summary of the lecture.
- Follow up and get full reference details of any recommended reading, links and cross-references given by the lecturer. Check the module website for these references and any other information posted after the lecture.
- Discuss the lecture/material content with other students.

Try it out for yourself

Try out some of the strategies and tips given in this chapter by watching part or all of an online lecture from an open courseware site. Good sites for this are:

www.academicearth.org   www.openculture.com

www.TED.com   www.freevideolectures.com

www.khanacademy.org   www.learnerstv.com

www.Utubersity.com

25 Tools, technology and note-making software

It's worth thinking about the pros and cons of the different physical mediums and tools you use to make notes. There is one important point to note: regardless of which tools you use, *they should not be a replacement for good quality reading, thinking, selecting and note making*. The act of note making and the use of tools can give you the illusion of thinking and studying effectively – but it is how deeply you think about things and the 'what' and 'why' of your notes that is most important, not the pen, paper or software you use.

With this point in mind, below is a list of tools you might choose to help you make notes, with some useful points and tips. As with the note-making styles outlined in Chapter 23, you can use a combination of tools to suit your individual note-making needs and context.

Note-making tools

Pencil, pen and paper

If you write on paper, use punched A4 pages so that you can organise them into a file or folder later. Pencil is good as you can rub it out, and one advantage of writing by hand is simply to practise legible handwriting.

Notebooks and journals

Notebooks and journals are useful to carry around and they keep your notes together in one place. However, you can't then reorder the pages, unless you use only one side of the pages and then cut or tear them out. If you use a notebook (or indeed any type of paper), put your name and a contact number on the front or inside cover so that you can be contacted if you lose it.

Index or note cards

Index cards are small cards of stiff paper used to record a single idea, theme or piece of information. They are called 'index cards' because they are often used to store information in a particular order. 'Note cards' is a more general term.

Using index cards might sound old-fashioned, but they can be useful because they encourage you to have only one idea on each card and therefore to stick to the main points (cards are particularly useful for noting key terms and concepts, theories and models). If you tend to make too many notes, you can go through your cards after making your notes and reject cards that are not relevant.

Cards are particularly good for reviewing, ordering and reordering information to suit different purposes, such as building an essay plan. You can even shuffle the cards and lay them out randomly to encourage new and creative ways of thinking. Cards are also useful for building up an ordered research retrieval system and for reviewing notes generally. Disadvantages of using cards are that you are restricted to small amounts of information on each card and that you need something in which to carry them.

Make sure that you leave a small space at the bottom of each card to add source information, cross-references and your own comments.

Front of card

Oswald AJ (1997). Happiness and economic performance. *The Economic Journal* 107(445), 1815–31.

Date of notes: 19/1/2013 p. 1827

Evidence that economic progress only marginally affects happiness

Back of card

4   main pieces of evidence:
- Reported happiness in US – only fractional ↗ post-war
- Europe – only slightly higher levels than 20 yrs ago
- No. of male suicides > in nearly all Western countries since '70s
- In UK and US job satsfctn has not increased (where data is available)

Computer files

Among the many advantages of computer files is the save, search and share functionality. You can also add your own notes to existing text files and PDFs. However, there are still situations where it is difficult to take or use even mobile devices, or where typing is inappropriate or disturbing, so it is also worth thinking about the various paper options listed above.

There are three main disadvantages to using technology:

▶ You can't quickly and easily flick through all your notes, although this is improving as software functionality develops.

▶ You can temporarily or permanently lose data through no fault of your own, so *make sure you back up files*, even if you use cloud storage.

▶ You need to be careful when sharing notes online. Even if your notes contain only information from a text, they are still likely to reflect your own personal selection and prioritisation of this information. Giving someone your personal notes and comments before you have completed the relevant assignment might lead to intentional or accidental plagiarism between you and the person with whom you have shared, and it is *your* responsibility to ensure that this does not happen.

Citation and reference management software

You will probably have free access to EndNote, RefWorks or EndNote Web to search, copy, store and manage your references and to build up your personal research record. These programs are easy to use and very useful, so ask for a demonstration from your university library or study centre. You can also use social bookmarking software such as CiteULike, Furl and Delicious (think about whether you want to share your references) or other bookmarking software such as Google Bookmarks (not the same as bookmarking as it saves whole searchable text in the cloud).

Note-making software

You can use software such as Evernote (free), OneNote or the note-making tool on PDFs to make linear, Cornell and table notes. You can also annotate documents using track changes or similar free tools.

There are quite a few good software downloads for making pattern and visual notes and for mind mapping, including ExamTime, Inspiration, XMind, SimpleMind, FreeMind, VUE and MindGenius. A free way of making basic mind maps is to use the *Illustration*, *Shapes*, *Text Box*, *Clip Art* and *Drawing Tools* functions of Microsoft Word.

Presentation software

Some people make notes using presentation software such as PowerPoint, Present.me or Prezi.

Digital and smart pens

There have been great advances in these pens over the last few years and although they can seem expensive, they are worth investigating if you need to make lots of notes by hand. Digital pens such as MyScript Studio (Notes Edition) are used with special paper to record and upload what you write, and smart pens such as Livescribe also record sound.

Speech-to-text software

Programs such as Audio Notetaker record what you hear and convert it into a written text that you can colour code, rearrange, change and annotate. Bear in mind that this is not the same as making your own notes, and that copying word for word what someone has said into your own work without acknowledgement is a form of plagiarism.

Summary

▶ Experiment with different note-making formats and vary your note-making style according to your reasons for making notes, the subject matter and the type of material.

▶ Use a combination of different note formats and tools as appropriate.

▶ Face-to-face lectures and seminars are crucial parts of your course, and you need to make the most of them by preparing beforehand, making meaningful notes during them, and doing the follow-up work afterwards.

▶ Experiment with different note-making tools (pencil and paper, software, recordings, digital pen) but remember that the quality of what you note down and of the thinking that underlies your notes is much more important than the tools you use.

MAKE THE MOST OF YOUR NOTES

26 Review and rework your notes

Always review your notes. Research shows that students who look back over their notes to check for clarity and meaning, and who reflect on their notes, are more successful learners. Research also shows that the sooner you review your notes the better, so try to do this within a day of making them.

Reviewing your notes doesn't mean just reading over them; it means engaging with them. Similarly, collecting information is not the same as thing as learning or having knowledge – you need to do something active and creative with your information. So, reviewing and actually reworking your notes should always go together and you should use your notes to extend and develop your understanding of your subject.

Review your notes

▶ Look at your notes as if they were written by someone else to see if they make sense and give a clear picture of the main point(s) and order of importance.
▶ Fill in gaps and correct any errors you know you have made.
▶ Use a dictionary or subject glossary to look up any words or terms you don't understand.
▶ Highlight or underline key points.

Rework your notes

▶ Use a different format: from linear to pattern notes or vice versa, or from mind map to table.
▶ Write a short summary – what would you say if a friend asked you to explain your notes to them? This will help you to clarify your understanding and improve retention of information.
▶ Review your notes on the topic from previous weeks and look for connections and similarities or differences between different ideas, arguments, evidence and viewpoints.
▶ Use your notes to write a short critical reflection.

Writing a reflection can be extremely useful. It can be informal but it's a good idea to write in your own words, in full sentences and to use quotation marks for exact phrases from the text. Include a short summary of what you have learnt (if the text has a diagram or data, try to summarise this in one sentence) and also include your thoughts from your questioning and evaluation of the text.

A reflection will help you to restate the author's information and ideas in your own words and will enable you to further develop your own thoughts. It will help you to see how the text or lecture fits in to the wider picture of your subject and to relate what you have read to what you already know. Finally, a written critical reflection will help you to see why, how and where you want to use your source in your assignment.

An example of a short reflection

Oswald argues that economic performance *does* affect people's happiness but only because it influences employment rates. He argues that it is whether people have a job or not that has a significant effect on their well-being, not income. I think that this is a very interesting finding and not one I had expected. I can see how this would be the case but I think that Oswald is exaggerating his claim. His evidence has some flaws in it and his finding that 'Unemployed people are very unhappy' seems to me to be over-simplified. The data he uses in fact only looks at men and also does not say that people without jobs are **very** unhappy. Also, I know some unemployed people who are very happy!

Still, Oswald is clearly an authority in this field, has published widely and the background notes give details of where I can find more evidence for his claim. I will probably use this article as a main source in my essay but I will check out more closely some of the data Oswald uses and will also try to find authors that have other perspectives and argue against him.

....

- Reorganise your notes around your assignment question title, adding comments and identifying any knowledge gaps.
- Reorganise your notes around your own unique question or angle to help develop your own 'voice'.
- Use your notes to write an annotated bibliography (see p. 152).

Look after your notes

You will need to refer back to your notes for months if not years, so keep them organised and safe from physical damage or loss.

Accidental collusion

- **Collaboration** is when you are *explicitly* required to work with others. Keep a record of what you have shared with the group and make sure that your final assignment clearly states what collaboration took place.

- **Collusion** is when you work with others in a hidden way and is a form of cheating. Be careful not to accidentally take part in collusion – don't lend your notes or other written work to other students if you are supposed to be working individually.

Accidental plagiarism

Be sure to always show clearly when you have used words *and/or ideas and information* from your reading. Even when you express information completely in your own words (paraphrasing), you *must* give a reference both in the body of your assignment and also in the bibliography.

Be careful not to imply that you have read something when you have not! If the article you read by author X mentions author Y, you must put something such as 'Y cited in X' in your assignment to show that you have only actually read the article by author X.

Misrepresenting the author

If you use an author's argument in your essay, don't use their material out of context. Be aware of how the bit you are using fits into the author's whole argument and present this context clearly. For example, you would be misrepresenting Oswald if you said that he views economic growth as not important.

Don't let your sources take control

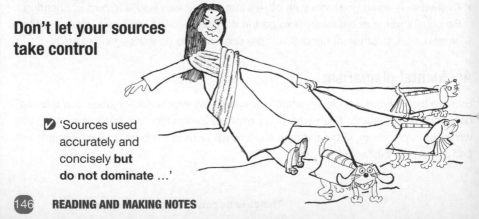

☑ 'Sources used accurately and concisely **but do not dominate** …'

Avoid writing an assignment that consists mainly of large chunks of written-up notes sewn together by only thin threads of your own sentences. Try to make *your* argument and voice stand out as the dominant one, and make your notes work for you as evidence in support of *your* answer to the assignment title. Your aim is to meet the expectations and marking criteria at the top of the well-built assignment wall:

> 'Evaluates evidence and synthesises materials clearly to develop persuasive arguments.'
> 'Evidence used appropriately to support their conclusion.'

Summary

▶ Students who have a clear purpose for making notes, who separate out more important from less important information, and who use their own words, are more successful learners.

▶ Notes should *not* be chunks of slightly changed copying, but the start of the process of expressing your own 'way of understanding'.

▶ Experiment with different note formats and try using more than one format for different stages of your reading and note making.

▶ Writing a short reflection from your notes will consolidate your reading and thinking and will maximise the effectiveness of the whole reading and note-making process.

▶ Notes that directly address your assignment title and your own questions in your own words, and that include your own comments, can almost act as the first draft of your assignment.

▶ Develop a sense of ownership of your notes. It should be *your* voice your tutor hears when reading your assignment, and developing your own voice should start at the note-making stage.

Final comment

I hope that you have found this pocket guide useful. Anything worthwhile you read should have an impact on other aspects of your life and on your world view. Believe it or not, writing for academic work does involve creativity, and if you have an active and engaged approach to reading and note making you will be surprised at the new and creative thoughts and questions you can generate.

Appendix 1: Answers to exercise on reliability of sources in Chapter 8

Ananthaswamy A (2004). Eat less and keep disease at bay. *New Scientist*, 2444, 11–12.

New Scientist is a magazine and is not peer reviewed so not reliable and not academic.

Davies R, Roderick P and Raftery J (2003). The evaluation of disease prevention and treatment using simulation models. *European Journal of Operational Research*, 150(1), 53–66. [Accessed 26 January 2014]

A scholarly journal so reliable and academic.

Health Development Agency (no date). *Coronary heart disease: guidance for implementing the preventive aspects of the National Service Framework.* http://www.nice.org.uk/niceMedia/documents/chdframework.pdf [Accessed 26 January 2014]

A government report and so reliable, although you should try to find the publication date to check how current it is. The report will not have been peer reviewed and so is not strictly academic.

UK Essays (no date). *Prevention of CHD in the Indian population.* http://www.ukessays.co.uk/essays/nursing/prevention-of-chd.php [Accessed 26 January 2014]

Not authoritative, not reliable and not academic.

Appendix 2: Examples of common abbreviations for note making

Full word or phrase	Abbreviation or symbol	Full word or phrase	Abbreviation or symbol
and/plus	+	maximum	max.
approximately	approx.	minimum	min.
because	∵	minus	−
compare	cf.	number	no. or #
decrease	↘	pages	pp.
different from/unlike	≠	regarding	re.
for example	e.g.	results from	←
government	gov.	results in/leads to	→
greater than/more than	>	same as/ditto	"
important	imp.	similar to	≈
in other words, namely	i.e.	therefore	∴
increase	↗	versus	vs.
information	info.	very	v.
less than/smaller than	<	with reference to	re.
like/equal to	=		

Appendix 3: Definitions of words used in this guide

acknowledge To indicate that a source has been used and to give information on that source. A common way of acknowledging an author is to give a reference (see below).

annotated bibliography A brief summary and evaluation of a text that comments on the author's background, the context and intended audience of the text, and its value and contribution to the subject.

annotation A comment, explanation or additional piece of information added to a text.

article A separate piece of writing in a larger publication. Common types of articles are newspaper articles, magazine articles and academic articles in academic journals.

cite, to To mention (and usually give information on) an author. A common way of citing is to give a reference. The word *citation* is also sometimes used to mean a quotation.

primary source The first, original source of information or ideas.

reference Information about a source. You give a reference in your assignment (an in-text reference) and also in your reference list.

secondary source A source which writes about, discusses or uses a previously written primary source.

References

Food Standards Agency (2013). *Front of pack food labelling: joint response to consultation.* Page 30.

Oswald AJ (1997). Happiness and economic performance. *The Economic Journal* 107 1815–31.

Neil Fleming's VARK model: www.vark-learn.com.

Useful resources

Cottrell S (2011). *Critical thinking skills*. 2nd edition. Basingstoke: Palgrave Macmillan.

Cottrell S (2013). *The study skills handbook*. 4th edition. Basingstoke: Palgrave Macmillan.

Godfrey J (2013). *The student phrase book*. Basingstoke: Palgrave Macmillan.

Godfrey J (2013). *How to use your reading in your essays*. 2nd edition. Basingstoke: Palgrave Macmillan.

Godwin J (2012). *Studying with dyslexia*. Basingstoke: Palgrave Macmillan.

Godwin J (2014). *Planning your essay*. 2nd edition. Basingstoke: Palgrave Macmillan.

Monash University Learning Support. http://www.monash.edu.au/lls/llonline/study/.

Oxford Brookes University Upgrade Study Advice Service. http://www.brookes.ac.uk/services/upgrade/study-skills/a-z.html.

Perdue University Online Writing Lab (OWL). https://owl.english.purdue.edu/owl/.

RMIT University Study and Learning Centre. http://www.rmit.edu.au/studyandlearningcentre.

The Open University Skills for OU Study. http://www2.open.ac.uk/students/skillsforstudy/.

University of Southampton Study Skills. http://www.studyskills.soton.ac.uk/.

Williams K (2014). *Getting critical.* 2nd edition. Basingstoke: Palgrave Macmillan.

Index

assignment title
  assignment 1, 22
  assignment 2, 23
assignment titles, understanding, 21–3
  concept words, 21
  function words, 21
  scope, 21

critical thinking, 83–7
  assumptions, gaps and flaws, 85–7
  context, 85, 89
  develop your understanding, 88–9
  evaluating, 87
  locating texts in the subject, 88–9

learning styles, different, 121–2
lecturer comments and marking criteria, 20
libraries, university, 44–6

myths about academic writing, viii–ix

notes, making, 87–139
  abbreviations and symbols, 151
  critical reflection, 142–4
  examples
    poor, 112
    good, linear, 108–10
    good, pattern, 111
  formats, 115–22
    Cornell or split page, 109, 117
    linear or list, 116
    mind maps, 119
    paragraph, 117
    pattern, visual, nuclear, 111, 118
    table, 120
  from lectures and audio-visual, 123–31
  having a purpose, 97
  key features, 101–3
  reasons for making notes, 13–14, 98
  reviewing and reworking, 141–7
  secretary syndrome, 105–6
  software, 132–8

technology, 132–8
tools, 132–8
top tips, 104–7
notes, using, 145–7
    accidental plagiarism, 145–6
    collaboration and collusion, 145
    controlling your sources, 146–7
    misrepresenting the author, 146

peer review, 39–40

reading
    active reading, 1–5
    building stamina, 6
    close, 55
    differences between school and university,
        1–2
    environment, 62–3
    flexibility, 58–9
    gist, 54–5
    methods, 53–9
    order, 53
    planning time for, 60–1
    questioning and evaluating, 65–87
    reasons for, 7–12

scanning, 54
screen or paper, 57–8
speed, 61
reading lists, 27–32
    Economics and Happiness, 30–2
    Nutrition and Lifestyle, 27–8
    things to remember, 25–6, 33
reading lists, off-road search
    for assignment 1, 35–7
reading problems
    difficult sentences, 93–4
    difficult texts, 91–2
    difficult words, 92–3
    feeling confused, 90
reading texts
    accurate understanding, 81–2
    active reading, 1, 65
    argument, 71
    description, 70–1
    explanation, 71
    finding the key message, 66–72
    language clues, 78–80
    opinion and argument, 72
    text extract 1, 68–9
    text extract 2, 74–7

research log, 51
reviews, abstracts and summaries, 48

scaffolds, 6
search engines, databases and websites,
     41–2
searching beyond your reading list, 34–7
  off-road search for assignment 1, 35–7
sources
  academic sources, 38–43
  fine-tuning your selection, 47–9
  key questions for sources, 49
  off-road, 34–7
  online sources, 41–2
  reliable sources, 38–43
stages of using your reading for an
     assignment, 18

text extract 1 on nutritional labelling 68–9
text extract 2 on happiness and economic
     performance, 74–7